THE
Eventual
MILLIONAIRE

THE

Eventual

MILLIONAIRE

HOW ANYONE CAN BE AN ENTREPRENEUR AND SUCCESSFULLY GROW THEIR STARTUP

Jaime Tardy

WILEY

Published by John Wiley & Sons, Inc., Hoboken, New Jersey.
Published simultaneously in Canada.

For general information on our other products and services or for technical support, please contact our Customer Care Department within the United States at (800) 762-2974, outside the United States at (317) 572-3993, or fax (317) 572-4002.

Wiley publishes in a variety of print and electronic formats and by print-on-demand. Some material included with standard print versions of this book may not be included in e-books or in print-on-demand. If this book refers to media such as a CD or DVD that is not included in the version you purchased, you may download this material at http://booksupport.wiley.com. For more information about Wiley products, visit www.wiley.com.

Library of Congress Cataloging-in-Publication Data:

Tardy, Jaime.
    The eventual millionaire : how anyone can be an entrepreneur and successfully grow their startup / Jaime Tardy.
        pages   cm
    Includes index.
    ISBN 978-1-118-67470-3 (Hardcover); ISBN 978-1-118-67487-1 (ePDF); ISBN 9781118674741 (ePub)
        1. New business enterprises—Management.   2. Small business—Growth.
3. Entrepreneurship.   I. Title.
    HD62.5.T359   2014
    658.1'1–dc23
                                                                        2013039713

Printed in the United States of America.
10 9 8 7 6 5 4 3 2 1

*To all of the Eventual Millionaires out there,
and to my husband and children who wear their
Eventual Millionaire T-shirts proudly.*

Contents

Foreword

Dan Miller

New York Times *best-selling author of* 48 Days to the Work You Love

Ah yes, "If I were a rich man." That familiar plea from the popular show and movie *Fiddler on the Roof* seems to echo the wish and the dream of many today. If only I were rich, then I wouldn't have to go to work every day. And yet, when we talk to those who are rich, getting out of working hard doesn't appear to be their goal at all. The money was not the primary goal at all. Rather, money showed up because the person wanted to do something worthwhile and thoroughly enjoyed the work they were doing. *The Eventual Millionaire* is a fresh reminder that ending up wealthy is not a position reserved just for the lucky or those born into the right family. It is available for anyone—but may not come in the way portrayed in movies and fictional stories.

And thus we jump into some observations that challenge *common* thinking:

- We can't go after money directly—it will stay just out of our reach. It seems money is a by-product of combining our skills, talents, and a reasonable economic model.
- We don't become millionaires by being envious of those who already are. Rather, we become millionaires by thinking like millionaires think—and they tend to be not greedy and jealous, but extremely generous.
- We don't become millionaires by hoarding resources so we can eventually "give back." Instead, it appears millionaires have been giving back from the very first day.

- We don't become wealthy by caring for only ourselves, but by caring deeply for everyone we meet.
- We don't become millionaires by hoping to be lucky, but by acting on opportunities that others ignore.

When I was just 13 years old, my life was dramatically impacted by a little recording by Earl Nightingale called *The Strangest Secret*. The message presented was essentially the time-honored principle "We become what we think about," but it struck me at an impressionable time and became a critical building block of my life. I learned the power of feeding my mind positive, hopeful, and optimistic thoughts as opposed to allowing the challenges of a legalistic religion and a poor farm life to determine my attitude and future. And I learned that by taking responsibility for my thinking and actions I could determine the direction of my life. I discovered we can all choose to tell our life story as a victim or as one who has chosen to walk in success and abundance.

Nearly all of us dream of and wish for lives of happiness, meaning, fulfillment, and riches. And yet, it seems that reality assures us that we will experience hardships along the way that make a straight path to those benefits nearly impossible. It seems nature's way is for us to grow from the unexpected struggles that inevitably show up. But like the butterfly struggling to get out of the cocoon, our struggles are part of the process of making us fully alive. And like the butterfly, those struggles are not intended to limit or cripple us, but to allow us to develop our resilience, fortitude, compassion, personal excellence, and wealth-building insights. The millionaires Jaime has interviewed describe that process over and over again. They did not avoid those struggles but chose to believe there was light on the other side.

You'll see that if you take action, you don't have to wait on someone to pick you for success. You pick yourself. If you blame, point fingers and make excuses, you'll block any chance for financial success. But you can open the floodgates by taking full responsibility for where you are, and can create the future you want, starting today.

Jaime observes that millionaires don't think ideas are worth much. It's true—ideas are a dime a dozen. But a person who creates a clear plan of action to go with a great idea can change the world—and his or her bank account.

For Day 47 of *48 Days to the Work You Love*, I recommend that the reader take a millionaire to lunch. I get more feedback about being stuck on that step than any other. But most people simply never ask a millionaire to lunch, believing that those who are already successful are now unwilling to help those a little further behind. *The Eventual Millionaire* shares story after story of how that is not true. Millionaires are quickest to offer help and be available. As Guy Kawasaki shares, they are not obsessed with making or holding on to their money or belittling those who are struggling. "I don't think the goal should be to make a million dollars. I think the goal should be to make the world a better place, increase people's creativity or productivity and I think that making a million dollars is a natural outcome of successfully changing the world."

In Chapter 5, Jaime talks about the power of *Mentors, Masterminds, and Networking*. Yes, we all would love to sit down with the millionaires of the world to learn how to follow in their footsteps. Fortunately, I have had the privilege of doing that for many years. So how did I happen to be in the right place at the right time to do that? I wasn't. But like you, the reader, I had easy access to their books, audio programs, seminars, blogs, and podcasts. You are now in their company as well as you turn the pages in this book.

I commend you on taking advantage of this intimate look inside the thinking, attitudes, and beliefs of millionaires. This is not another get-rich-quick book; it is realistically titled *The Eventual Millionaire*. But by modeling the behavior of those you are about to see in these pages and with *Continuous Forward Motion*, you, too, can put yourself firmly on the path from which there's no turning back—you *will* become a millionaire.

Acknowledgments

These are my thank-yous. I know it's a bunch of people you don't actually know, but think of how much you would want others to read it if your name was here!

(And I'm so sorry if anyone is left out of this; I will buy you a coffee to make it up to you.)

First, the entire community of Eventual Millionaires. You are why this book is here. I thank you from the bottom of my heart for your comments, and your e-mails, tweets, and Facebook shares! Especially my insiders group, which selflessly helped with the creation of this book.

I need to thank all of the millionaires I interviewed who have given me their time, and wisdom. I truly appreciate every second I have spent with them and now I am lucky to call many of them my friends. Thank you so much.

My amazing husband, Matt, whose support is insane, who cleaned the house, watched the children, and let me go write by the lake whenever I wanted. (I couldn't ask for more!) The best children in the world, Finley and Jet. One of the reasons why I am doing what I love is to show you that you can do it too. My family, Mom and Dad, Ryan, Dave, Garrianne, love you!

To all of my friends who helped me along, whether I was complaining, or excited, editing, or in research mode: Kurk Lalemand (my mentor), Kim Napolitano-Perry, Shae Bynes, Amanda Johnson, Tatum Rebelle, Ginna Caldwell, Natalie Sisson, Kate Northrup, Chris Ducker, Harry and Donna Harris, and my amazing mastermind group, Pat Flynn, Todd Tresidder, Roderick Russell, and Jeff Rose. You all rock!

Introduction

First Things First

How This Book Came to Be

From the time I was little, I wanted to be a millionaire. At the time, I didn't know why; I just knew it was important to me. By the time I was 22, I seemed to be in the right direction. I had a $250,000 house with a pool, nice new cars, and the facade of success. Everything looked amazing on the outside.

But the reality was I hated my job, and I was miserable. I was traveling constantly, working 60 hours per week, and had gained more than 25 pounds from going out to eat all of the time. In addition, I wanted to start a family, and I knew that my current job situation would not be right for that. To make matters worse, my husband and I were $70,000 in debt, and I was the primary bread-winner for our then two-person family.

It was under these conditions that I took the first major step toward building a new, fulfilling life for myself. I created a plan to pay off the debt so that I could quit my job and pursue work that I enjoyed. With a strict budget, many life changes, and the complete and total cooperation of my husband, I achieved those goals in 16 months.

As I already mentioned, I had a lifelong goal of becoming a millionaire. But I had to put that goal on hold while I learned to live a new life that wasn't all about the money. After quitting my job and having my first child, I was pretty sure that I wanted to be an entrepreneur. I experimented with many different business ideas before reaching the point where I am now.

After much trial and error, I became a business coach, and after years of working locally with clients, I launched a website called http://EventualMillionaire.com. I was back to thinking about millionaires again, but this time, it was from a learning perspective. I'd already learned some hard lessons about happiness and money. After learning how to go after the money the wrong way, my new goal was to learn how to have happiness and money.

Interviewing these millionaires has afforded me more knowledge about money and happiness than I ever dreamed of. And by sharing the interviews with the world, I feel that I'm also providing a service to others who desire the same knowledge.

This book is a culmination of all that I've learned since those days when I was unhappy in my job. This is the book I wish I'd had during that time. My hope is to now share with you a way to avoid the mistakes I made so that you can go straight to a place in your life where you can enjoy happiness *and* wealth.

What Is a Millionaire?

Technically a millionaire is simply someone who has a net worth of a million dollars or more. The typical perception is that millionaires have everything they could ever want. And, that they are successful and happy. What do you imagine when you think of a millionaire? Do you think of Wall Street executives, celebrities, fast cars, or yachts?

Many people think they could have all of that, too, if only they had a million bucks! But even for most millionaires, money is not the top priority. In fact, for most of them, money is just a nice side benefit. After interviewing more than 100 millionaires, I've discovered some key insights into what makes millionaires successful and what makes them happy.

I want to change the way you think of a millionaire, I want you to realize that you can be an Eventual Millionaire. I want you to start being an Eventual Millionaire now.

You Don't Need Money to Find Meaning

When I was working in the corporate world I worked in the cable industry, providing video on demand. I remember one day I was working in another state and, I'll admit, I was freaking out over some of the issues that had just cropped up. It was up to me to fix them, and I wasn't sure that I could do it, but I had to. My stress level was *high* because the problems had to be fixed *now.*

A coworker came up to me, seeing me stressed, and said, "Jaime, it's just cable TV, it's not like we are curing cancer."

That was my wake-up call.

We only have one life here on this Earth, yet we tend to forget that fact all too often. We tend to let the minutiae of our lives take precedence. We need to put things back in perspective.

You don't need to be a millionaire to have the lifestyle you want. In fact, you probably don't need anywhere close to a million dollars to have the lifestyle you want. Most of us just want to enjoy our work and contribute to the world. What we don't want is to work at a widget factory that doesn't seem to make this world any better.

Why figure out the lifestyle first? Why don't we just work our butts off for a lot of money and then have a ton of time to enjoy it? Because I can tell you from experience, you won't be happy.

When you make it all about the money, everything suffers.

Removing My Goal

I gave up my goal of being a millionaire while I was figuring out how to love my work. During this time, it wasn't about the money but about getting to a good place in life. My goal was to find something I loved. I wanted my own business that would grow into something bigger. I wanted to find something where the income was not capped, I wanted to help people.

Only later, after finding the work I loved, did I realize I could add that goal of being a millionaire back. However, I want to do it on *my* terms. I wanted to live this life to the absolute fullest, retire with dignity, and do amazing and wonderful things. I wanted to become a better person by learning to deal with challenges. I wanted to help more people.

That means it may take longer for me to become a millionaire. Heck, I could have done it much faster if I had kept my previous job. But enjoying every day was more important than that goal.

> The biggest mistake that I had ever made in my career was sacrificing my marriage, my health, and my kids to try to make money.
>
> —DANI JOHNSON, MULTIMILLIONAIRE SPEAKER

Your goal might be different. You might not need to create a million-dollar net worth or business. Maybe you just want the freedom that six figures affords you. Then you can save your million even if it takes longer. The person who dies with the most toys doesn't win the game. In fact, we aren't even looking to win the game. We are just looking to make progress; to make our skills better than they were before, and to help as many people as we can in the process.

CHAPTER

Are You an Eventual Millionaire?

After you become a millionaire, you can give all of your money away because what's important is not the million dollars; what's important is the person you have become in the process of becoming a millionaire.

—Jim Rohn

After interviewing more than 100 millionaires, I can easily say that there are patterns to success. So many similar stories and struggles have come up in the course of years of studying them. I can also easily say that calling them *millionaires* almost seems trite, because they are utterly amazing people, and their net worth does not define them. I'm lucky to call many of them my true friends.

At the beginning of this study, I thought like most people think, that millionaires were somehow different, that they had something that "normal" people didn't have. I asked questions like, "Did you always know you would be a millionaire?" because I was trying to figure out if they were born with something most people don't have.

Are You an Eventual Millionaire?

An Eventual Millionaire is someone with a goal to become a millionaire, eventually. But Eventual Millionaires want to do it on their own terms, with an enjoyable life and an enjoyable business.

Eventual Millionaires put the *process* of making money into perspective. Usually overachievers, they are willing to work hard. But they don't want to sacrifice their daily lives for their goals. Eventual Millionaires are smart. They want to enjoy the process of making money, not just the end goal (that is, the money).

There are different stages of being an Eventual Millionaire. You might be stuck in your day job, knowing that there is something more that exists for you. Or you might already be on your path, and started your own business, but you need to take it to the next level.

Quiz: Are You an Eventual Millionaire?

If you say yes to most of these questions, you are an Eventual Millionaire, too!

1. Do you consistently think of ideas to earn more money?
2. Do you usually care about value and spend less than you earn?
3. Do you already feel successful in many things, but aren't sure if you can do something on your own?
4. Do you know you are destined for great things, but feel like things aren't moving fast enough?
5. Have you always wanted to be in control of your own time and experiences, but right now feel like you are just trying to get by?
6. Have you tried business ideas that didn't work out before, but still have the passion to try new ones?
7. Does the idea of working for someone else the rest of your life scare you?
8. Does having a boss feel constricting, and you don't want someone telling you what to do?
9. Do you hate the idea of waiting until retirement to enjoy your life and the world?

10. Do you believe that success and wealth are in your power, but don't want to rely on others?
11. Do you want to travel more but don't have enough vacation days?
12. Are you able to daydream about what you want to be when you grow up, no matter how old you are?
13. Do you only sleep four to five hours per night because you are too excited about your new ideas or business?
14. Do you read success stories and think, "What made them so successful? How come I haven't made it yet?"
15. Do you want to do work that matters, not just something that pays well?
16. Do you want to become a better person through personal growth, even if it's hard?
17. Do you want to leave a legacy?
18. Do you want to give more, but feel unable to right now?

If you answered yes to at least half of the questions above, you are most likely an Eventual Millionaire! You want to forge your own path, and have the freedom of time and money. Most importantly, you want to be doing something you truly enjoy, too! You are already successful in many areas of your life, even if you don't feel like it. (Eventual Millionaires tend to have high expectations!)

Even if you said no to more than half of these, keep reading. Maybe you haven't thought about owning your own business yet, but you'll soon discover why becoming a millionaire through business might be your best bet! And don't worry if you don't feel like you can do it yet. Many millionaires felt the same way.

Having Happiness and Wealth Is Possible

In this book, you'll learn:

- How to put your life first (which means taking control of your money and how you live).
- How to find work you truly enjoy.
- How you can get over your fears, excuses, and limiting thoughts (just like millionaires have done!).

- How millionaires start their businesses the "right" way.
- How to keep moving forward even when there are road-blocks in your way.

And the best part is that you'll read stories of millionaires who started off just like you.

The Journey Is the Fun Part

As an Eventual Millionaire, you'll want to adopt the mind-set that you are on a journey to becoming a millionaire. Thus, the process of making money—the fulfilling work that you choose to do—will be your journey.

And as with any journey, there will be challenges. But really, would life be any fun without challenges?

When I was younger I loved video games. One time I was playing a game called *The Sims*. It was a real-life simulation where you have a house and can buy furniture and upgrades. I thought the game would be much better if I had more money. I didn't want to do the work, so I found a cheat that would give me an unlimited amount of money.

I was excited. I bought everything I wanted. It was fun! However, 20 minutes later, I realized that the game wasn't fun anymore because there was no challenge. Suddenly, there was no point.

Each person is different. What is important is finding out what deeply fulfills you. What journey, what work, is going to make you happy? What challenges are going to make you feel alive and motivated? What type of work are you still going to enjoy after you've met your financial goals?

Obtaining money can temporarily make people feel alive when they are struggling to make ends meet. But money can become meaningless once you have all you need. I know this might be hard for some people to believe, but it's really true. Think about it, if you love chocolate, but had to eat it every day for every meal, would you still love it?

(I've tried it before by the way, and even I, a chocoholic, felt sick at the thought of eating another piece of chocolate.)

Just like with the video game example, your goal should be to find work you love to do just for the joy of doing it. The end result—winning or "the money"—should be secondary.

Love the Process from Thousandaire to Millionaire

We tend to value experiences we can look forward to. We tend to appreciate things more when we don't experience them on a daily basis.

Do you remember Christmas—or whatever holiday you celebrate—when you were a child? I thought the holiday season was amazing, and I couldn't wait for it to come. I wanted those presents *so badly*. The build-up was intense. I remember the letdown the day after Christmas, when the glamour of the day had worn off and I no longer had anything to look forward to. I had the presents, which were nice to play with at first, but lost their luster quickly.

As an adult—especially if you have children—you realize that it's not about Christmas day, but about the whole process of the holidays. It's the buying of presents, the parties, the lights, and the traditions that are the true joys of the holiday. Christmas morning is the apex of it all, but as an adult, you really enjoy the whole process of getting there.

That's what your journey to a million should be about: enjoying the whole process. The only thing that will happen on your goal date will be that you change your title from "thousandaire" to "millionaire." That day will be special, but you'll realize when you arrive that the time leading up to it was actually the whole point of it all, not the goal.

It's Okay to Love Money

I'm going to say something now that might make you uncomfortable. Are you ready? Wait for it . . . *I love money*. I really do.

I've asked a lot of people this question: "Is it okay to love money?" Almost all of them have cringed. They said things like, "I love the options that money can give me. I love the things it can do for me. But I don't love money."

Google "define love" and you will see that love is:

noun: An intense feeling of deep affection: "their love for their country."

We can say "I love my country" or "I love my house," so why can't we say that we love money, too?

Realize I'm using it as a slang word; I don't want to debate the meaning of love.

I do, however, want to stick with the term *deep affection*. That being said, the love for your children or spouse or family is a deeper type of love than how we love our smartphone or washing machine.

I am not saying that you should love money more than people, but I do want to crush the weird aversion we have toward saying we love money.

Money is a tool. Just like my washing machine or just like my house. Money makes things easier. I love my washing machine. I used to have to hand wash all of my sweaters. I now have a great washer and dryer that have a hand-wash cycle! It makes my life so much easier, and for that I am thankful. If it were to be taken away completely, I would be upset, frustrated, and it would make my life harder if I had to hand wash the amount of laundry I have at my house.

There is a distinction we need to make. Loving money is okay; however, putting the love of money above people or priorities is not okay. Whether you call it love or not, if you put making money above respect for others, you lose in all ways.

We sometimes think that Love for Money = Greed, but that's not the case at all. Greed is an intense, selfish desire. Greed causes you to be only concerned with your own profit or pleasure. That is putting your desires without the consideration of others ahead of all else.

I believe that you should love money because with love comes respect. Our culture needs to respect money more.

Our emotions toward and relationship with money rise and fall with the numbers in our bank account. You get paid, you are happy. Then you spend it. At the end of the month you feel bad because there isn't any money left.

We should look at money as if it were a tool. We need to lessen our emotional attachment to it. We should just appreciate it.

You should be the ruler of your money. The money shouldn't dictate your worth or your feelings that day or week or month. Many of us think our lives are missing things, and we assume it's money. Money gives you more choices, which is why we equate money with freedom, but it can take a lot less money than you think. It's not necessarily the money itself that offers freedom, but people often use it to fill a void inside. The first step toward freeing yourself from money is to figure out how to live your life with the least amount of money necessary. After that the addition of money will be an additional happiness—not the cause of the happiness.

From APA.org, the website of the American Psychological Association:

> If you hear someone say "money can't buy happiness," say "give me yours," Gilbert a researcher from Harvard joked. People with money enjoy better nutrition, can go places with loved ones, worry less about their children, and have more freedom to set their own schedules, he said. But money's ability to buy happiness levels out for people in the United States, with huge increases in happiness for people who vault into a middle-class income of $40,000 to $70,000. Once that level is reached, increases in wealth generate smaller rises in happiness.

I want to help you put money back in its place. A place where *you control the money and money doesn't control you. Where money becomes an additional happiness, not the sole source of happiness.*

Money Does Not Make You Rich

I know that most people think of a millionaire as a person with a lot of money. But I want to say that the million dollars does not make millionaires rich, at least not the ones I have interviewed. They are rich for many other reasons besides the money.

The millionaires I have met are amazing people. Some of the sweetest, kindest people I've ever met. It didn't matter what their net worth was. In fact, when you go after the money solely, and assume that the million will change things, you can become sorely disillusioned. One of the millionaires I interviewed, Todd Tresidder (from FinancialMentor.com), said:

> Once I became a millionaire it was this big "so what." I mean it led to one of the most unhappy periods in my life and I couldn't really understand why. I had just so many false assumptions in my brain about what it was to be financially independent and what was the basis of happiness and what really leads to happiness and so it really sent me back kind of to ground zero and I started reworking this stuff.

I think everyone who wants to contribute more to the world should have a goal to be a millionaire, not for the money, but for five benefits:

1. More millionaires with morals.

We need more millionaires who are not greedy and have solid morals and integrity. We need the moral millionaires to outweigh the greedy ones. We need you to step up. I once heard someone say, "If you want to save the rain forest, buy it." Having money and influence is a good thing, especially when your integrity shines.

2. A comfortable retirement.

Because of inflation, by the time I am 65 I will need at least $2.4 million to live comfortably ($50,000 per year) at retirement. Can you imagine people who are millionaires yet live a middle class lifestyle in retirement? In 1950, a loaf of bread was 12 cents. Now a loaf of bread costs $2.49 (2010 statistics). That is more than 20 times the cost! Imagine how much groceries will cost when you retire—$20 million will be the new million. Isn't that crazy? So the good news is that each day with inflation you are getting closer to a million. The bad news is, no one will care about millionaires, and everyone will want to be a billionaire!

3. Grow your mind-set.

I believe that part of the reason why we are on this earth is to make it better; to make progress. I also believe that it all starts with *you*. As humans we don't like to push past our comfort zone. It's uncomfortable! We will stay within our normal comforts unless there is a bigger reason not to. You need that bigger reason. When you become a millionaire you grow. Resistance bubbles up when you are trying to do bigger and more amazing things. As you do bigger things, you will grow because you will be forced to deal with confidence issues, self-worth issues, control issues, communication issues, disappointment and failure, and on and on and on.

4. Achievement.

A million is a benchmark on how much value you are putting out in the world. If you are working with integrity, especially if you are in your own business, the amount of revenue you generate relates to how many people you are impacting. If your business helps people with their finances, imagine how many people you are impacting if you are generating a million a year in revenue. It's scarce, too; there are not many people in the United States or in the world who are millionaires.

5. You have more to give.

I surveyed my audience of Eventual Millionaires. I asked them why they wanted to become millionaires. The most common response was not to go on a trip to Paris, or buy a huge house. The overwhelming response was to help more people. Imagine how much more you can help. How much more of an impact you could make. You can create so much more with the resources that would open up to you.

If you are an Eventual Millionaire you are probably already giving. Keep on making as much of an impact as you can. One millionaire I interviewed used to sponsor a child. Once her business took off, she sponsored 100 more. When I spoke to her recently, she said she was in India helping personally.

So that is what I want. I want you, the person who has integrity and truly cares about people and making this world a better place, to become wealthy. Not just so you can enjoy your own life, but also because I know you will be helping others enjoy theirs, too.

> A wise man does not accumulate for himself. The more he uses for others, the more he has himself. The more he gives to others, the more he possesses of his own.
>
> —LAO-TZU (c. 550 BC)

The Most Common Way People Become Millionaires

Now that I've explained why you should still want to be a millionaire after you've found your fulfilling work, it seems like the next step should be explaining how people actually becomes millionaires.

What is the one proven way to become a millionaire? Is it investing? No. Real estate? No.

Even though you will find many gurus in those areas teaching how to become a millionaire, based on the research from Thomas Stanley in *The Millionaire Next Door*, more millionaires have made their money by owning their own businesses. The millionaires I've interviewed have proven Stanley right, too. I interviewed millionaires who are first-generation rich, and own their own businesses. That's why this book is so heavily focused on starting your own business, too.

Here are a few of the many millionaires who have made their money through entrepreneurship:

- Brad Deal had the typical American middle-class family. Then one day, his daughter saw a bench in the park and said it looked like a letter of the alphabet. That was the inspiration to start his company called Sticks and Stones, which creates custom wall art using the images of letters from nature and architecture. His products have been in *O* magazine, and one piece was even given to Tom Cruise and Katie Holmes as a wedding present.
- Craig Wolfe, owner of CelebriDucks, has been everywhere in the media, including the *New York Times*, with his rubber duckies that look like celebrities.
- Doug Guller hated corporate life, but failed at his first startup after college. He decided to get a job, save money, and try again. In less than seven years, he had more than 12 restaurants and 800 employees.
- Hanny Lerner, owner of Mod Restoration, started her business by doing a Groupon, even though she didn't provide the services she was offering. She gained 95 new clients right away and outsourced the work.
- Joy Gendusa, owner of PostcardMania, was a graphic designer and was trading time for money. She knew things

had to change and she wanted to have more time to spend with her kids. After trying a postcard company and having extreme frustration with them she decided to start her own. PostcardMania now does more than $19 million in revenue.

Now You Start

How you spend your days, and what you contribute to the world, matters. So why do we give that all up in the pursuit of money?

Don't get me wrong. This book is called *The Eventual Millionaire*. The money matters, too. But you should strive for a life where you can make decisions based on what's best, not on whether you have the money. Life first, then money. Make sense?

Just hoping that the future will be bright won't get you anywhere. Hope is a wonderful thing, but it isn't enough. That allows the future to smack you in the face. Instead, you want to go out and find the future you want and step into it.

You *can* change your life—especially if you know what you need to do.

I know from interviewing amazing, successful people in both life and business that nothing was just handed to them; opportunities arose, and they seized those opportunities. Those same opportunities could have fallen by the wayside if they hadn't risen up to meet the challenge.

Are you rising up to meet the challenge presented to you now? Do you have a plan for your work, your money, and your future?

We have so much we want to do in life, and yet it always seems like we have until tomorrow to do it. I'm here to tell you that the time is *now*.

Let's Get Started!

You can start right where you are. First answer these questions:

- Are you happy with your current work, but struggling to get your finances in order?
- Do you have a good business idea, but need help with implementing it?
- Do you need to find a new type of work—something that really makes you feel alive?

- Do you need to get more connected with others in your line of work?
- Do you need help finding a mentor?
- Do you have fears that are keeping you from taking the next step in building your business?

If any of the above questions apply to you, please keep reading!

In the following chapters, I show you how millionaires have dealt with challenges such as the ones listed earlier, and I'll help you deal with yours, too.

Let's do it!

CHAPTER

Start Working with the Money You Have Now

Your money or your life.

—Joe Dominguez

Your money and your choices make up your life. You may not want to admit how much control money has, but the choices you make with your money determine what you accomplish. Money can give you freedom, or make you stuck. You have the power to change your future, and it all begins with your money. You want your money to work for you; you don't want to work for your money. I know, because I learned the hard way.

In my early and mid-twenties, I was just doing the best I could. I wasn't quite sure how my husband and I always felt broke when we made really good money. On top of that, I wasn't happy at my job at all, because I wasn't in control. I was a project manager for a company that installed computer equipment for cable companies, so if there was ever an issue with that equipment (day or night) I would be called. I would receive a call on Friday and find out that they needed me to fly out on Saturday to deal with a disgruntled customer.

I spent so much time and energy trying to make sure people never had issues with their cable. Ironic because I didn't even watch TV! I was spending so much time and mental energy on something I didn't even care about and longed for the freedom to do something I cared about. I wanted to *matter*.

I felt stuck, because I knew we were in debt and I couldn't quit my job because of the choices I had made. I had hoped things would just work themselves out on their own because I couldn't be honest with myself. I didn't want to look at how bad our debt situation was.

Finally, after deciding it was more important to take control of my debt and face my fears, I knew it was time to take charge. It was that moment that it all changed. I realized that I was the only one who could change my situation. We weren't going to win the lottery. I needed to be the hero of my own story. If I didn't lead a life that mattered, it was by my own choice, not because of circumstances I couldn't control.

Facing Debt Head-On

To get a handle on our debt, I first had to find out just how much we owed. I remember the moment of adding up all of our debt so clearly. I was on my computer and looking up the bills online. I had a little piece of paper where I was writing the numbers. It hurt to write them down.

> Student Loan 1: $3,400 . . .
> Student Loan 2: $22,780 . . .
> Home Equity Loan: $24,560 . . .
> New Honda Civic: $19,300 . . .

Those numbers looked big on their own, and I didn't want to add them up. I hesitated, but I persisted. We were $70,040 in debt. Ouch. And this was even after we paid off the credit card debt! We used to put a lot more on credit (our whole $3,000-plus honeymoon!) but we had paid it off and stopped using them before.

I still felt humiliated; I thought I must be stupid because of the bad choices I made. I sat staring at the numbers in disbelief. I was 24 years old. How did I let myself get into all that debt so quickly? All of my life choices had seemed like smart decisions at the time, so why did I feel so stupid now?

The numbers truly shocked me. Though I was vaguely aware that I had a certain amount debt, I had no idea that they added up to be so much. We were responsible, had just paid off our credit-card debt, and had one car paid off already, so I had been feeling pretty good.

At that moment, I realized that those decisions I made earlier were holding me back now, and I couldn't quit my job to start a family because of how much we owed. On top of the loans and car payments, we also had a $240,000 mortgage. I made two-thirds of our household income, so I wasn't even sure that if we paid off all of that debt that we could live on one salary. We would probably have to sell our house.

Even though I was still reeling from the shock, I knew the first step for us was to start to control our money—to figure out where exactly the money we did have was going, and to figure out different ways to bring more of it in. That meant I had to learn a whole new way of doing things. I started to read everything I could find, from debt pay-off stories online, to books with step-by-step plans. I read every guru. I asked friends and family what they thought. I wanted to get out of debt as fast as humanly possible for two reasons. First, it's not fun scrimping and saving, and second, to start a family and quit my job.

Now flash back to just two months earlier when my husband and I were shopping for a new car. It was November and cold in Maine, and we were looking for something that would be pretty good in the snow and would work as a family car, because we knew we were going to be trying to have a family soon. We decided to trade in our Jeep Wrangler that we loved, but didn't deem family-worthy.

We researched for hours. We test-drove so many cars. We are a bit picky—we wanted one that looked cool but was great on gas and could handle all of the family stuff we needed. We finally decided on a brand-new Honda Civic. It seemed like a safe and logical choice. It wasn't terribly expensive, around $19,000 new, and the payments were manageable.

I loved this car, all the way to the cool digital speedometer. When we drove it home, I imagined bringing a little baby home from the hospital in it. I imagined being a soccer mom and driving the kids around. I felt like I was becoming prepared for our baby.

But in reality, I was doing the opposite. I was putting our family further into debt, which was taking me away from the future I had envisioned for myself. After adding up our debt, even though the car was brand new, I knew it had to go and even though we had put so much time and effort into researching it, and I dreamed of bringing a baby home in it, it was time to say good-bye. What made that even harder is that my husband didn't want to get rid of it. He thought we would lose too much money. It only had a thousand miles on it.

It turns out that the old adage that the car drops in value the second you drive it off the lot wasn't completely true. Yes, we did lose some money, but it had only decreased in value by a thousand dollars.

Was the decision easy for us? No.

Was it worth it? It was one of the best decisions we ever made.

We ended up buying a $7,700 car, so our debt was cut down to $59,440. This gave us some big forward momentum. That first big push inspired us to keep going. We sold an off-road vehicle with 36-inch tires that was my husband's baby. He had worked on it for hours and was part of our local off-roading club. That brought in about $3,000 and allowed us to start an emergency fund of $2,000 and start to pay off the smallest student loan. I felt like $2,000 was enough for any small emergency, so we wouldn't have to use credit cards for anything.

A month later we found out we were pregnant. It was March 2006, and we were due in December. Our countdown had started! Our debt by now was down to $55,440, but we had to keep figuring out new ways to save money if we wanted to be out of debt by the time our baby was born. When I learned I was pregnant, my goal officially became to quit my job in nine months so that I could be home with my baby.

Even though I never wanted a monthly budget, we started one—and quickly realized we needed to cut it to the bone. I didn't think we were crazy spenders, but it all adds up quickly! We found cheaper car insurance and lowered our cell-phone plan. That left our budget to cover only the necessities like groceries and gas, and $25 each of our own spending money.

Having $25 a month for myself was not much money—especially because we decided that haircuts should come out of that fund! Needless to say, I think the only haircut I received that year was at the local cosmetology school. I would buy the cheapest tea at Starbucks when I went out, but that let me feel like I could still go out.

Sticking to the grocery budget was the hardest in the first month. We guessed that we should only spend $300 a month on groceries. Before setting our budget, I had never had to count how much money I was spending at the grocery store. I tried to keep a calculator with me while I shopped, but I felt dumb walking around the store with it; I felt like everyone was watching me. Eventually we figured out ways to make grocery shopping on a budget less of a chore. When my husband and I both went shopping together, we played a game to see who could add up the items in their head and guess the total grocery bill. It became a challenge to beat my husband.

We never went out to eat, but instead found that some of our friends felt bad for us and would pay for us to go to dinner with them. I hated to feel like we needed charity, and I told them over and over that we had the money—we just didn't choose to spend it on going out to eat.

Another discovery I made was that not only was gas so expensive, but it adds up so quickly! I knew it hurt going to the pump and paying a lot, but what I didn't realize was how much our driving was costing us. Before setting our budget, we would go out to the mall whenever we felt like it, or we would just drive without thinking to pick up something small from the store. One day I actually figured out how much it cost to drive to the mall—more than $10 just to drive back and forth! If we did that weekly, that was $40 a month!

So we started to reduce our trips. We planned out everything we needed to get all at once, and if we forgot something, we didn't make an extra trip to pick it up. It was annoying to feel like every time I drove the car I was wasting money, but every time we drove past a gas station and didn't have to fill up was a relief.

The only problem with not driving as much was that it was not fun being stuck in the house. I made it a goal to get creative and figure out a way to get outside without spending any money. We would go hiking or go on picnics. I always looked up inexpensive or free date ideas such as things going on in the community. That helped me see the task of saving money as an enjoyable one, and that way, I kept reminding myself of the reason I was doing it. This wasn't a punishment; it was a choice.

While all this time we made good money, I had a tight timeline. Because I wanted to be home with my baby and we only had so many months, we did everything possible to make extra income. I found out that if I flew out to a customer's location for work I would make $40 extra each day, and my food would be covered by my expense account, so I traveled as much as I could. I was working almost 70 hours per week when I was seven months pregnant! I wouldn't advise such drastic steps to anyone else, but I was determined to accomplish the goal I had set for myself.

My husband, meanwhile, had a sporadic income as a performing artist. He started doing website design and graphic design on the side to make extra money. He took any job that he could and was working literally day and night on extra projects. (He worked like a dog for those months and dealt with a very pregnant wife, so I commend him for what a great job he did!)

The clock ticked on—we had three yard sales, and sold a kayak, a wine rack, my weight bench, and more on Craigslist. We cleaned out every closet and sold random things on eBay. We started to realize how much stuff we had and how much stuff we didn't need. We thought we were minimalists before . . . but we were wrong.

I had my son on December 11. I was paid 60 percent of my salary for six weeks, and I took 12 weeks off. I figured out that if I went back to work for two and a half months, then I would be able to pay off the student loan and still have our savings of $23,000, which I hoped would last a year.

I went back to work for a little more than two months and did not travel at all. My husband started to book a lot more work than he had in the past. In April 2007, when my son was four months old, we became debt-free. We paid off my student loan and still had that $23,000 in the bank. Once our tax refund came back, we were even able to buy a great family car with cash. We were debt-free, I was able to be home with my beautiful boy—and we had our family car again. It gives me chills now realizing how everything worked out.

The Debt-Free Rules

Beware of the little expenses. A small leak will sink a great ship.
　　　　　　　　　　　　　　　　—BEN FRANKLIN

I learned a few rules when I was climbing out of more than $70,000 of debt—things that I didn't know before but that have truly shaped my life now. I see these same rules show up in the way millionaires talk about money.

Rule #1: Get Honest

There are a couple of platitudes that just don't apply to finances:

Ignorance is bliss—*wrong*.
What you don't know can't hurt you—*wrong*.

Ignoring your finances is so easy. It's normal to only pay attention when the next bill is due, or when you realize your bank account slipped below $100. People spend countless hours planning events like a wedding, yet it's rare that the same amount of time is spent figuring out your finances. And unlike one fleeting day, your finances impact every day throughout your entire life. Why is it so common for people to ignore their financial situations?

Two reasons: We feel like it's too complicated or that we aren't smart enough to figure out how to manage money, and we are afraid of what we might find when we open the Pandora's box of our bank statements.

But you need to be honest. Being honest doesn't just mean don't lie about it. Being honest means admitting those things that you don't want to admit, uncovering things that don't want to be uncovered, and remembering things you don't want to remember. Like when I kept ignoring that my home equity loan had a variable interest rate and kept climbing up and up.

Listen to Your Inner Critic Listen to what the voice in your head says when someone brings up that they are debt-free or doing well financially. Does it say one of the following?

"Yeah, Yeah . . . I don't want to hear it."

[Sarcastically] "Lucky them!"

Or, "Wow, I could really learn a lot from them."

The quick judgments in our head explain a lot about how we truly feel. Paying attention to those thoughts and assessing where they come from is what being honest is about. One reason we become jealous or brush off hearing about others' financial successes is because we compare ourselves to them. Whenever we make a comparison, one person always comes out the loser. Stop putting yourself in a losing battle. Change your focus from comparing to learning.

One way to start to change your perspective is to pay attention to the impulsive thoughts you have about money. Think about budgeting. What are the first thoughts that come to mind? Do you think people with budgets are financially responsible, or does this make them cheapskates? If you have a knee-jerk reaction toward the negative, then that may be a sign of some insecurity about your own financial situation. The first action you can take in being honest is to become more aware of your inner critic. You can't move forward until you do.

How to Be Honest   If you are going to become debt-free, you are going to have to be honest. Believe it or not, there are people out there who are doing much better with their money than you are. And on the flip side, realize that there are many who don't have money to eat.

Being honest is accepting where you are now, exactly as you are:

Accept that you have been misinformed about money and have made mistakes.

Accept that you will not be 100 percent perfect with your money all the time and that is okay.

Accept that you can make the decision today to make progress.

Accept that you are the only person who can get yourself out of this mess.

Accept that you may be jealous or envious of others from time to time.

Accept that in order to move past that jealousy or envy, you have to be honest with yourself.

Do you accept? If you can accept these in your gut, you can move forward. Be honest with yourself, and you'll find that you will become the hero of your own story.

Rule #2: Be Value Conscious

One common theme with the millionaires I've interviewed is that they invest in things that are high value. I don't mean investing like trading stocks. I mean investing in anything we spend money on.

There is a big difference between spending and investing. Spending is paying for goods or services. Investing is paying for goods or services *with the expectation of gain.*

This means the return of value needs to be higher than the price. How do we figure out what has a high value? Are things that are more expensive inherently more valuable than less expensive things? Frank McKinney, a millionaire and best-selling author, drives a Yugo. In fact, it's a "presidential blue 1988 Yugo." Although he could buy a very expensive car, he doesn't, because he doesn't value it. But he does value other things, like spending money for his charity in Haiti.

Many millionaires know the value of a dollar. They know because many of them have been broke. Here is what Frank McKinney said about starting with nothing: "When I came to south Florida, I had a 50-dollar bill in my pocket. I just wanted a job. I was very proud to have that first job digging sand traps on a golf course earning $180 a week, but I always knew, subliminally, subconsciously, that there was a higher professional calling for me than digging ditches on a golf course."

Dani Johnson, a highly successful author and coach, said, "I was a broken, desperate, homeless person who had no confidence, who believed in nothing, who trusted nobody, and who didn't think I could succeed at anything."

MJ Demarco, another sought-after author, knew he wanted to be an entrepreneur but had to deal with the difficulty of not succeeding for years. He said, "I lived at home with my mother until I was 26 years old. I did all kinds of goofy jobs, from mopping floors in pizzerias, to delivering flowers, to delivering newspapers at 3 A.M.—all kinds of crazy stuff. But in the background I was always working on an entrepreneurial business."

What Do You Value?   Often enough we don't ask ourselves the question, "What do I value?" It's an instrumental question to figure out what you truly want. If you value freedom highly yet make the choice to buy a new boat that lands you with a monthly payment, you are not living your values. Most of the time, when you dig deep, it's not material items that you value. It's so much more than that. On the flip side, for example, if you value spending time fishing with your children, then buying that boat can be a great investment. As long as your spending reinforces your values, you are investing.

When I interviewed Todd Tresidder, creator of Financial Mentor, he said this: "My experience is that somebody who is valuing stuff over experience is trying to fill a hole in their lives. You have to identify that hole, and you have to understand it. I think anybody that's walked that path knows that stuff does not buy happiness.

"The easy way to understand it is that happiness is an internal experience, and any time you try to satisfy an internal experience with an external thing, you're doomed to failure. So everybody thinks that when they get a million that all their troubles go away. *That's the millionaire myth.* When you get a million, or you become what you consider financially independent, you've lost all your excuses for unhappiness. You have no excuse for being unhappy. Now you have to look yourself right in the eyes, and you have to know that it's you. Everything that's going on in your life is all about you. It's all about self-responsibility. You can't blame it outward anymore."

After I interviewed Todd about what he calls the *millionaire myth,* he then went on to talk about how becoming a millionaire led to one of the unhappiest periods of his life. He thought that being financially free would solve his problems. It didn't. The problems you have now might just be magnified with more money.

So if we don't need stuff, do we even need to be millionaires? That's a really good question. Maybe you don't need that much, but what would you need in order to feel abundant, maybe even rich or just really secure in knowing that you can do whatever you want? What we need to do is find out where you are now and how much you need. We'll have to do a net-worth analysis, but even before that, you need to know your starting point.

You may have heard some research that money doesn't buy happiness. That's incorrect. It does buy happiness, but the level of happiness only increases slightly even when the amount of money goes up substantially.

The correlation between income and happiness is positive but modest, and this fact should puzzle us more than it does. After all, money allows people to do what they please, so shouldn't they be pleased when they spend it? Why don't a whole lot more money make us a whole lot more happy? One answer to this question is that the things that bring happiness simply aren't for sale. This sentiment is lovely, popular, and almost certainly wrong. Money allows people to live longer and healthier lives, to buffer themselves against worry and harm, to have leisure time to spend with friends and family, and control the nature of their daily activities—all of which are sources of happiness.

—SMITH, LANGA, KABETO, AND UBEL, 2005

In "If Money Doesn't Make You Happy, Then You Probably Aren't Spending It Right," the authors start with the premise:

Wealthy people don't just have better toys; they have better nutrition and better medical care, more free time and more meaningful labor—more of just about every ingredient in the recipe for a happy life. And yet, they aren't that much happier than those who have less. If money can buy happiness, then why doesn't it? Because people don't spend it right. Most people don't know the basic scientific facts about happiness—about what brings it and what sustains it—and so they don't know how to use their money to acquire it. It is not surprising when wealthy people who know nothing about wine end up with cellars that aren't that much better stocked than their neighbors', and it should not be surprising when wealthy people who know nothing about happiness end up with lives that aren't that much happier than anyone else's. Money is an opportunity for happiness, but it is an opportunity that people routinely squander because the things they think will make them happy often don't.

Let's Start Spending Money in Ways That Make You Happy   Here are a few of the key principles that researches have found that make you happier. I correlated this data with the data I found, from paying off all of my debt and from the millionaires I interviewed.

Principle 1: Buy Experiences Instead of Things   Just as with Todd's example above, buying experiences makes us happier than buying "stuff."

One thing I realized when I was overspending on material items was that the "high" of buying new things would wear off quickly.

Once I bought that new thing I really wanted the happiness derived from it would wear off completely. Which is why we need to keep buying more and more to keep experiencing that same reaction.

Researchers found that the happiness derived from experiences instead of things wears off slower. Plus, when we go back and think or talk about the experience, we gain happiness from that. It's like we get more bang for our buck with experiences over material stuff!

Principle 2: Help Others Instead of Yourself   When I surveyed my followers to find out what was the reason they wanted to become a millionaire the results were surprising. The most common answer wasn't freedom or even experiences, it was by far, "To help others and give more." We feel like if we have more money and time we will be able to give more.

The research shows that whenever we improve our connections with others we are happier. Helping others or spending money on others fulfills that. The funny thing is we don't recognize it. Most of us don't predict that we would be happier spending money on others, which may be a reason why we don't actually do it as often as we want to!

Principle 3: Buy Many Small Pleasures Instead of a Few Big Ones   Does eating one 12-ounce cookie give us twice the pleasure as eating a 6-ounce cookie? Studies show the answer is no.

In fact, eating two 6-ounce cookies give you more pleasure than eating one 12-ounce cookie. Why?

Because the amount of pleasure you get lessens after the initial act. That means when you go on a buying spree and spend $100 that initial act of buying gives you pleasure and then diminishes. But if you spent $10 separately 10 times you would derive more pleasure.

That means that breaking up or separating into smaller pleasures will give you more happiness!

> If money doesn't make you happy, then you probably aren't spending it right.
>
> —Elizabeth W. Dunn, Daniel T. Gilbert,
> and Timothy D. Wilson

Principle 4: Pay Now and Consume Later We live in a society that loves "Consume now, Pay later." If you can experience the purchase without having to wait, why not?

Well, apparently we get more happiness from the opposite.

Consume now, pay later eliminates anticipation, and anticipation is a source of "free" happiness. The person who buys a cookie and eats it right away may get X units of pleasure from it, but the person who saves the cookie until later gets X units of pleasure when it is eventually eaten plus all the additional pleasure of looking forward to the event. Research shows that people can reap substantial enjoyment from anticipating an upcoming event even if the event itself is not entirely enjoyable.

Isn't anticipation an amazing source of free happiness? Just like I mentioned before, do you remember when you were a child, and you would look forward to a holiday like Christmas or your birthday? Remember how excited you were? (And if you don't remember, talk to a child in your life who has a birthday coming up. The anticipation will be palpable!)

Action Item: Finding What You Value

Think of the last 10 items you bought. Write them down (including things like going out to eat, or entertainment, or material items):

1. _____	6. _____
2. _____	7. _____
3. _____	8. _____
4. _____	9. _____
5. _____	10. _____

After you purchased each of these, you probably had a feeling about whether it was worth it. You probably had a feeling in your gut about it. Think about that feeling. Was there guilt for spending so much on something that wasn't really worth it? Or are you still elated with the purchase?

Mark an X next to the items you still are very happy you bought. Now look at those items. If you have more than three, narrow them down to the top three. Now, this isn't an exhaustive list, but it will start to give you an idea of the things you value. How will you cut out or cut down those items on your list that you bought but don't value?

Rule #3: Numbers in Your Head Don't Count

I talk with many people who know their finances. "Knowing" is not enough. The *Merriam-Webster Dictionary* defines the difference between knowing and understanding:

> **To know** is to have a practical perception of something. "He knows his finances."
>
> **To understand** is to achieve a grasp of the nature, significance, or explanation of something. "He understands his finances."

To understand one's finances means that you understand the meaning behind the numbers, not just the basic figures themselves. We all need to seek to understand our finances.

How do we understand our finances? Well, the basics include having our numbers written down, like income and expenses (also known as a budget!). But bigger than that, understanding your finances means knowing what those numbers mean to your life and goals. If you keep that expensive cable TV, what are you giving up for it, or, to put it another way, what can't you have because of it? What can you sacrifice now to make your dream vacation a reality next year? When will you be able to quit the day job you hate?

The First Number: Your Net Worth   Have you ever figured out your net worth? Your net worth is all of your assets minus all of your liabilities. This is simple math, just addition and subtraction. It just takes some time to find all of the numbers. The first time I did it, mine was negative. How far away from a million are you?

Seeing the difference between your total net worth now and a million might feel like you have to climb Mount Everest to get there. But at least now you know where you stand. The numbers were still a reality before you knew them!

This part of my journey actually made me feel a bit better. The first time I figured out my net worth I was in a college class and for homework I found out that I had a net worth of –$50,000. When I did it again while I was almost done paying off my debt, I realized that I had a net worth of about $100,000. Even though I was in debt, I still had made some progress. I knew I had about $900,000 more to hit my goal. It seemed big but it gave me a goal.

The Second Number: Income and Expenses (A Spending Plan!)   Next in understanding your finances comes from knowing how money flows in and out of your life. In business this is called *profit and loss,* and it's vital for success. In our personal lives, we call it a budget, and it has such an undeserved negative connotation!

Five years ago it felt like I was saying a four-letter word when I told people that we were on a budget. You might want to call it a spending plan, if that makes it easier on your family or others involved. Truly it's just about being very value-conscious about what you want and don't want to spend your money on.

I actually found a budget to be very freeing. I didn't have to feel guilty about the things I purchased anymore. In fact, right before writing this chapter, I did my budget for the month. No matter how much money you have coming in and going out, I firmly believe that understanding your finances is vital to having a healthy relationship with money.

Table 2.1 shows a sample budget. There is no replacement for taking the time to do it. I'm sure you have heard of budgeting before, but this time commit. Try it for three months. Slog through the hard stuff and just take some action on it.

All that's involved here is entering what you pay right now for each of the categories. You need to understand your finances and what you typically spend money on now, and then we can work on creating more overflow.

You may not know what all of your extras are yet. I used to go to Target and walk out having spent $100, and then a week later I wasn't able to recall anything I bought except for a mop. When you're just getting started, it may take saving your receipts and figuring out what you are currently spending to get an accurate picture.

The Third Number: Your Current Spending   The final pieces of information you need is how close your current spending matches your budget. It's never going to be perfect. But if you plan on spending $400 on groceries every month, how do you know you did it? That's where the tracking comes in.

If you were to come to my house and look at my refrigerator, you would see what I like to call my Fridge Sheet. I am a geek and love my apps and computer software, but I still like the

Table 2.1 Sample Budget

Giving			Funds		
	Giving			Personal Fund	
	Other			Personal Fund	
Housing			**Medical**		
	First Mortgage			Health Insurance	
	Second Mortgage			Life Insurance	
	Real-Estate Taxes			Doctors Bills	
	Homeowners Insurance			Dentist	
	Repairs or Maintenance Fee			Optometrist	
	Other			Drugs	
Utilities			**Personal**		
	Electricity			Child Care	
	Water			Babysitter	
	Gas/Heat			Toiletries	
	Phone/Internet			Pool	
	Phone			Hair Care	
	Cell			Education Adult	
				School Tuition	
				School Supplies	
Food				Subscriptions	
	Restaurants			Gifts (including Christmas)	
	Grocery			Miscellaneous	
Transportation					
	Car Payment		**Recreation**		
	Car Payment			Entertainment	
	Gas and Oil				
	Repairs and Tires		**Debt**		
	Car Insurance			Payment	
	License and Taxes			Payment	
	Car Replacement			Payment	
					Total

Table 2.2   Monthly Spending Form

Out to Eat	Groceries	Gas	Jack	Jill	Kids	Pets	Entertainment	Extra
$	$	$	$	$	$	$	$	$

old-fashioned method of writing down my expenses. I like seeing my expenses in front of me every single day.

It's a really simple form. It looks like the one shown in Table 2.2.

You enter the amount you budgeted in the current month in the very first row. Then any time you spend anything, you subtract it. It's pretty simple!

After the month ends you will have a clear picture of how much you actually spent and how much that compares to what you budgeted. You may be a bit over or a bit under depending on what came up that month, but it should be very close. If it's off too much one way or the other, you know how to make it better for next month.

I have many years of budgets, and I can go back and see how much I've spent each month. That's a really helpful financial tool, because it tells me how much my budget was off. That allows me to go back to every July for the past few years and see how much I'd actually spent. This is what small businesses do with their budgets too. Budgeting helps you become very clear on your spending habits so you can start to predict what the future will look like. That means that if in July we usually tend to take a family vacation, then I would be able to start planning and saving for it months in advance.

There are also amazing tools online to help you with this. I started with spreadsheets because I was overwhelmed by the digital options. Now I use Mint.com for my budget, and it's connected to my accounts so it automatically records my spending. It gives you a chance to create budgets, and it will e-mail you if you overspend in one of your categories. It's a great tool that I highly recommend.

Rule #4: Control Your Money

Now that we have all of the important numbers, your net worth, your income and expenditures, and your current spending, this is where we put together a plan for them, which includes what to do with excess money. I know you might be saying, "Excess money? I don't have a lot of that!" But that is the goal. The goal at first is to reduce your expenses and increase your income so that excess amount gets bigger.

Get Rid of Expenses   Take a hard look at those expenses. What can you cut? Sometimes it's easy to just go ahead and cut what you know you don't need. Other times it's really hard. Does giving up on Netflix really make a difference if it's only a few bucks a month? For questions like this, I go back to being value-conscious. If you truly value watching movies, ask yourself these questions:

> Can I give it up for a short period of time?
> Can I do something that is cheaper (e.g., two Redbox movies a
>   week is cheaper than Netflix)?
> How can I get the same enjoyment/value for less?

Ask yourself these questions for each expense. *And remember that these cuts are temporary.* The plan is to do what you need to do to take care of this. You need to dedicate yourself to create the best set up you can for moving forward on your goals.

Increasing Your Income   There are many ways to increase your income. I cover the three that worked best for us.

1. Selling things.

You probably have a lot of stuff you didn't even realize you had. I admitted that I had more stuff than I thought and when I actually let go I decided to get rid of things. We sold everything we could, from furniture that wasn't necessary, to old computer monitors, to our kayak. When you can start to let go of the excess stuff you own, you can start to feel better. You feel more organized, and you feel like you are in control of things.

As you downsize, it's important to show appreciation for what you do have. There are so many people with much less, even if you are living paycheck to paycheck. Taking old things and donating them to Goodwill or friends in need may not help your budget, but it will help your mind. Giving during a time of scarcity is a great experience.

2. Increase your wage at your current job.

I know the economy isn't great, but if you are providing a lot of value to your employer, it doesn't hurt to ask for a raise. I remember I was only three months into working at my company, and even though I was making more money than I ever imagined possible before, I asked for a raise. I even asked for a big raise. I'm not usually someone who enjoys risk, so it seemed a bit out of character for me. However, when I looked at the risk logically, I realized the worst they could do was say no. They had loved me as an employee so far. In fact, they hired one of my friends from college based on my recommendation. If they said no, then they would at least see my eagerness to improve. Although I was very nervous when the words came out of my mouth, just a few short days later, they said yes.

If you want to ask for a raise, here are a few tips:

Make sure you are going above and beyond your current job description already. Employers love to see eager workers and know that they have people they can count on. They don't want to lose people who are willing to go above and beyond.

Make sure there is no ultimatum implied. When asking for a raise, it may sound like you aren't happy with your current salary or that you are unhappy with your job. To keep things peaceful, make sure you validate that you appreciate your current situation, too. You can alienate your boss or company if they think you dislike the work and just want more money to justify it.

Go in prepared and use numbers. Make sure you go in knowing what you are asking for. Don't just say, "I want a raise." Your employer needs to know how much you are looking for. Use numbers to show how much value you are delivering. If your job has any direct relation to creating gross revenue, make sure you explain how much you are bringing in. If you have had a direct impact and have created happier customers or fewer problems with software, and so on, make sure you back up your claim with numbers. You want to make it a no-brainer for your employer to give you a raise, even if they don't have the funds to pay you now. This will give you a good chance to show how valuable you are.

If you don't feel like you have anything to show them to justify a raise, then go create more impact in your company before you ask for one. If you can't show your value to an employer, then don't ask for a raise. If your company is holding you back so you can't show your value, then ask them for more responsibilities!

3. Starting a business.

If your goal is to start a business, start it now as a side hustle. The next few chapters go over finding a solid idea and how millionaires started their businesses. Ahead, you'll also find help with goal setting and creating a three-month action plan.

You want the side hustle to start now so you can start to learn a lot about business while you have the security of your job. It also allows for more income so you can pay off your debt faster. That way you can set yourself up financially to quit your day job.

Action Item

Download the worksheets at http://TheEventual Millionaire.com for these four steps:

1. Figure out your net worth.
2. Create a budget and current expenses list. Use the worksheet or go to Mint.com and create an account.
3. Find expenses to cut.
4. Figure out a plan to increase your income (via starting a business or asking for a raise).

Money Beliefs

We all have beliefs around money that shape the choices we make with it. Common money beliefs are:

Money Beliefs

- Most rich people are vulgar and disgusting.
- Most rich people are not very generous when it comes to those less fortunate.
- The type of car a person drives is a good measure of success.
- The key to success is hard work.

- People who inherit a lot of money have it made.
- In business, everyone has his or her price.
- I feel that fate plays a large part in how wealthy a person becomes.

Money Values

- If I knew I wouldn't get caught, I might do something illegal if it meant a lot of money.
- I would rather spend and enjoy the best now, and worry about saving when I get older.
- If I had enough money, I would quit work and live a life of leisure.
- I judge how successful I am by how much money I make, relative to others.
- It's important that I wear expensive clothes.

Look through the above statements and look within. Do you have any of these beliefs or values yourself?

Just make a note in your head on which ones you might feel are true.

An interesting study compared these beliefs and values with our feelings internally like jealously, low self-esteem, and being status-seeking.

Here are the findings:

The Study Found:

Low self-esteem was related more consistently to money beliefs, and especially to the statement, "Most rich people are vulgar and disgusting."

Low self-esteem and the value that, "It is important that I wear expensive clothes."

Jealousy and the belief that, "Rich people are vulgar and disgusting."

Status-seeking and jealousy were more consistently related to money values, and most strongly with the statement, "I judge how successful I am by how much money I make relative to others."

It's difficult to tackle money beliefs head on, but if we can figure out how they relate to our sense of self we have a place to start.

For example, if in reading the earlier text you realize you have self-esteem issues, make it a point to get the book *The Six Pillars of Self-Esteem*, by Nathaniel Branden.

Once we can identify the piece within ourselves that can be adjusted we have the first step toward change!

From *Now* Onward

Make the commitment now to start working with the money you have now. Choose wisely things that will make you happier, get clear and honest with the real facts about money in your life, and start really controlling your financial life.

We need more people in the world who control their money, and less who have their money controlling them!

Stand up for your future and take the control back! It's the first step of being an Eventual Millionaire.

Debt-Free Rules Summary

Rule #1: Get Honest
Rule #2: Be Value-Conscious
    Principle 1: Buy Experiences Instead of Things
    Principle 2: Help Others Instead of Yourself
    Principle 3: Buy Many Small Pleasures Instead of a Few Big
       Ones
Rule #3: Numbers in Your Head Don't Count
Rule #4: Control Your Money

ACTION ITEM REVIEW

Action Item: Finding What You Value

Think of the last 10 items you bought. Write them down (including things like going out to eat, or entertainment, or material items):

1. _____   3. _____
2. _____   4. _____

5. _____	**8.** _____
6. _____	**9.** _____
7. _____	**10.** _____

After you purchased each of these, you probably had a feeling about whether it was worth it. You probably had a feeling in your gut about it. Think about that feeling. Was there guilt for spending so much on something that wasn't really worth it? Or are you still elated with the purchase?

Mark an X next to the items you still are happy you bought. Now look at those items. If you have more than three, narrow them down to the top three. Now, this isn't an exhaustive list, but it starts to give you an idea of the things you value. How will you cut out or cut down those items on your list that you bought but don't value?

Action Item

Download the worksheets at http://TheEventual Millionaire.com for these four steps:

1. Figure out your net worth.
2. Create a budget and current expenses list. Use the worksheet or go to Mint.com and create an account.
3. Find expenses to cut.
4. Figure out a plan to increase your income (via starting a business or asking for a raise).

CHAPTER

Millionaires Have Fears, Make Excuses, and Have Confidence Issues

We are separated by forces in society that give us the idea that we all have to appear totally competent, totally on top of things, totally together, as if fear doesn't factor into our lives.

—Tim Hamilton,
millionaire and owner of Astonished Designs

It's time to break down those forces. You see, it's easy to compare our internal thoughts of fear, lack of confidence, and struggle to the external images of amazingly successful people. Let's put millionaires and all successful people on a level playing field.

Do you want to hear that millionaires have "the exact same doubts" as you do? If you have fear, think about what your brain is doing to you. Your resistance to doing something uncomfortable or that scares you is running your life. ALL of us have fears. To be human is to fear. The difference between being successful or not is how you respond to those fears. So let's learn what fears millionaires have and how they've responded. Then you will see that they are very similar to yours.

That's good to hear, isn't it? The successful aren't immune to thoughts of fear and confidence issues. It's *normal* to have these thoughts and issues. But I've found out how millionaires recognize these issues and move past them anyway.

For example, fear pushes us to make excuses. Excuses like, "I don't have enough time," "I don't have enough money," or "I'm not good enough" will stop you from achieving anything. They hold you back. Millionaires have gotten very good at getting past their excuses. The key that sets millionaires apart from the pack is that they have the same doubts and fears as everyone else, but they have learned how to overcome their internal struggles.

What Fear Is

Fear is a wonderful thing. Repeat that in your head. Fear is a wonderful thing. It can save us from blundering into harmful situations. The problem is that our human bodies have not evolved fast enough to learn the difference between a legitimate fear reaction and one we should ignore. The problems we face each day are not life and death. When we get up in front of 100 people to make a speech, our physical reactions equal that of facing an angry buffalo. Even if you *feel* like you are going to die standing up there, chances are that would never happen.

So why does our brain do that to us?

Knowing what fear is inside our brain can help you understand that it's just a physical response, and while uncomfortable, it's nothing to be afraid of.

It's not about being fearless.

Science of the Brain

Our amygdala, which is close to the middle of our brain, deals with our emotions and fear. Our prefrontal cortex, which is right behind the forehead, deals with all the planning and the decision making. The funny thing is that they don't talk well to each other.

You can *know* logically that it doesn't make sense to fear in certain situations. Take people who are afraid to fly on an airplane. They know millions of people fly, they know rarely anything bad happens, but they can't get their amygdala to go along with it.

Before, if you saw a tiger you knew you needed to run. Your brain would automatically think it's a true threat. But most of us don't see tigers anymore except in the zoo. Because we don't have these huge life or death fears anymore, we morph our small nonlife or death fears into bigger problems.

Your brain doesn't recognize the fact that it's not a true threat. It might be a cat. A small cat that won't kill you, but that same fear response comes anyway.

The good news, says scientists, is that we're currently evolving right now. Those parts of our brain are starting to link up. It's just a *very* slow process. What I wanted to figure out was how do we make a shortcut between those two pieces of your brain so you can move forward anyway, even though you feel that fear? And does it matter that we get past our fears, or can we just accept them as a part of life?

Your Business May Fail If You Do Not Work on Your Fears

> Realize there is a force subconsciously at work in your mind that is tempting you to say no. The primary difference between my career and most others is that I don't let the fear that is there stop me. That is the primary difference.
> —FRANK MCKINNEY, REAL ESTATE DEVELOPER AND
> FIVE-TIME BEST-SELLING AUTHOR

When Dani Johnson—who writes and talks about getting the most out of your life—was younger, she felt like a failure. She was broke and pregnant at 17. She was a high-school dropout. Then she went to a conference and listened to four millionaires speak. Dani thought to herself, "Man, if I'm the dumbest person in the room, which I know that I am, and it takes me 20 years to figure this out and to learn how to do what they do, and if I fail to reach their income by 90 percent, then I would still do better in business for myself than I ever would staying at my job that I had at the mall."

You can hear the negative self-talk and the issues with self-worth she had then. But her logical mind knew that it was worth it to try entrepreneurship, despite all her fears. Dani now has five companies, is a multimillionaire, and an international speaker. Her internal game had to change in order for her to achieve all of those things.

Imagine she instead said, "What if I fail? I'm the dumbest person in the room; there is no way I could do it."

Her business, which now helps thousands of people achieve financial freedom, would not exist. She is changing people's lives every day because she overcame her fears.

Think about that for a minute. Your fears not only affect you, but also affect your family, your friends, and the people your business will serve. I am willing to bet that your children will be better off if you figure out how to face your fears, excuses, and confidence issues, let alone all of the charity and mentoring of our younger generation you can do once you have found success!

What Millionaires Think of Fear

I used to think that millionaires were superhuman. They do everything right. They know how to make the right decisions. They figured out something that I haven't yet or that other people haven't. They had to have innate abilities or skills to be better than most.

Now I don't think that is the case at all. I have millionaires who are in my mastermind group and some who are mentors. I have many friends who are wealthy.

They are just people.

They weren't born with the skills. Most of the skills that they have right now are completely teachable. One of the things they have, which I say over and over and over again, is that they have an immense desire to learn.

If you are reading this, that means you have a desire to learn, too.

Quotes from Millionaires

Amy Applebaum, success coach and creator, Release Your Inner Millionairess Coaching Club: "You start to move and decide that fear is part of the process. I know everyone is in fear. I mean I am in fear all the time because I am stepping out of my comfort zone."

Anita Crook, creator, Pouchee: "I won't say be fearless because fear sometimes is just a motivator, but take that fear and put it aside and follow your dream anyway. You're not too old, you're not too young, you're not too shy or too poor or too anything.

There are obstacles. We're always going to have obstacles but just put aside your fears and just go for it."

Sean Malarkey, online marketer and author: "Most of the time we are afraid. We have these fears that it's not going to work and it's not, so it's easier just to continue learning and feel like we're doing something that's going to help. But at the end of the day, a lot of it is fear driven. Just have no freaking fear and get it done.

"Most of the time, almost everybody I know that takes action sees good results or sees some results that's enough to let them know okay this is a great idea or it was stupid. Usually that nominal success will be so exciting to you or the fears are gone, at that point, and now you're really motivated to make it happen."

Derek Sivers, coach and author: "Abraham Maslow had a great quote that he said something like, 'Life presents us constantly with a choice between safety and risk' and he said, 'Make the growth choice a thousand times a day.' Reading something like that when I was 17 and just knowing him and his pyramid of self-actualization I kind of went all right.

"Again, that's like a rule of thumb or recipe for what to do and how to make your decisions in life. Make the growth choice a thousand times a day, okay, got it. I guess I kind of just run all of my daily decisions through that kind of filter."

Chris Gravagna, founder, Ondemandcolor.com: "I really think you need to channel your fear. Don't make it to where you are constantly second guessing yourself. Make it so that it allows you to take the protocol steps in driving to make sure that it's a great idea. Fear should allow you to do your due diligence. It should allow you to do the proper research. It should allow you to think twice before a decision and not second guess that decision 10 to 15 times because that consumes a lot of time. You know, I'm doing it, I'm not doing it, I'm doing it, I'm not doing it. It's also really important to have a good ratio of risk to fear and I fear that having a little bit of a higher tolerance of risk combined with fear makes for a good entrepreneur and you have a little bit more of a risk factor than a fear factor. That way you take that leap of faith that it's a good idea. Hopefully that fear allows you to do the due diligence which allows you to make an educated risk."

Now we know what millionaires think about fear. How do we actually deal with it? That's what you are here for! How do we step out of our comfort zone every day? We're going to go through four steps. Then you will learn tools and tips and tricks to get past the fear, since fear will definitely come up once you are getting out of your comfort zone.

The tips and tactics will help you in the moment. Realize though that facing your fears, and growing more confident is a journey. You will have small wins along the way, and you might not feel like you are making any progress. That's okay! Keep at it. Just like with everything. Keep moving forward.

Risk

Fear and risk play in the same sandbox together! Many times, if you feel like something might be risky fear will crop up. If you have ever thought about owning your own business, your risk meter might start rising (especially if you have a family to support!).

I really wanted to see what millionaires thought about risk specifically, because it seemed like they were taking much bigger risks than I was willing to cope with. It turns out, more often than not, they don't think of themselves as risky. They think of themselves as calculated. You can put the fear at bay when the risk is not so great that you cannot recover.

Crazy risk taking is not a trait of any of the millionaires. From interviewing more than 100 millionaires, I've found that they don't jump in without assessing the risk. It's also apparent that the risk they are willing to take coincides with their confidence in that area.

The amount of risk they are willing to take is a cumulation of confidence, mitigating their fears, and finding out if logically it can work. If this risk does fail, how big of a failure is it and can it be managed?

When you hear of people using all of their money, taking out loans, borrowing against their house or their retirement, that seems too risky! And most of the time it is.

David Heinemeier Hansson, creator of Ruby Rails framework and Base Camp, said, "I need to feel like we're moving in the right direction and that we're taking or making bets with good odds. I hate making bets that I consider to have poor odds. This is where I start to see the danger zone come in.

"That's why I never gamble. I know the house in Vegas has an edge over me. Why the hell would I participate in a game where I know that I am outmatched when I sit down at the table? So I sit down at tables where I have great odds. That doesn't mean I am guaranteed a success, certainly not."

This is what you should be thinking about. Make sure you play with good odds. The pressure that something too risky puts on you can *sometimes* be a good thing, but from most of the stories I've heard it mostly drives you crazy!

Frank McKinney, who does ultramarathons, talks about exercising risk like a muscle. It's something that can be strengthened. Your comfort zone can grow. You start to build up a tolerance and then it starts to become comfortable. I see this over and over again. That's why it's easier for serial entrepreneurs, even if there is big risk involved in the new companies. They have done it before. They have more confidence and more skill managing risks. That doesn't mean there isn't fear, but they mitigate that as well.

When I decided I wanted to quit my job, I took more than a year from making the decision to the actual leap. I had many things to line up beforehand. Paying off that massive debt for one! But also figuring out health insurance, and saving money. When I actually got the date to give my job the words I had been longing (and dreading!) to say, I had my bases covered. I was going into the unknown, but I knew I had reserves, and I did my best to leave on a good note. I left on such a good note, my employer let me know that I'd always have a job there if I wanted one. Now *that* is a good way to mitigate the risk!

Don't worry about not being able to take huge leaps of faith. You cannot bench-press 100 pounds when you never have before. Start slowly. If you have a big risk ahead, try to break it down into small chunks. See if you can do one bit at a time.

Confidence

Confidence plays a key role in any successful business. Low confidence can manifest in many ways. It could be that you aren't willing to charge what your product or service is worth. Maybe you won't speak to a business contact you need to because you are afraid. No matter what it is, every person in business has had aspects of a lack of confidence at some point in his or her career.

Excuses and fears arise when we don't know what the outcome will be, when we feel like we can't rely on ourselves to have our desired outcome. A lot of that coincides with being confident in you and your business.

> **Lewis Howes, information marketer and author of** *The Ultimate Marketing Webinar Guide:* "But if you can learn how to become confident with yourself, it takes a lot of personal development, like really looking inward and saying 'How can I grow every single day as a human to become better?', I think you are going to be able to build that confidence that way and the more confidence you have, the less fear you will have and fear is something that holds everyone back from becoming a millionaire, becoming anything they want to become because they're afraid to fail.
>
> "But when they have that confidence, they'll be less afraid to fail, more forward thinking on generating any type of results you want and that result will eventually come."

Confidence is: A feeling or consciousness of one's powers or of reliance on one's circumstances (*Merriam-Webster*).

When you are just starting in business you won't be certain about your own powers. That's completely normal! But please be aware that this is something that can grow with effort and time. Over and over again, millionaires have had to deal with lack of self-confidence.

The key difference between them and others though is just like I said earlier: They don't let that stop them! They continue to grow and get better. You need to make sure you can rely on yourself and your own powers. The way to do that is to keep relying on yourself over and over again so you start to trust yourself. Once that trust builds, your confidence builds.

It takes practice. The more practice you get in, the more times you step up to the plate, the more times you'll have to look back on to show yourself that you did it. That also means that practicing that sales call or practicing that presentation makes a difference, too.

Another piece that tends to play a part in confidence is how much you value the opinions of others. If you take others' opinions of you to heart, then either you will be too worried about what they think to even try, or you will be so focused on what others think that you can't be confident in what you think. If this seems to resonate with you, then this is a piece that needs to be worked on!

An opinion is not fact. Everyone has his or her own perception of reality. Just like asking eye witnesses to recount an accident, there will be differences based on their feelings toward the event. You will never be able to please everyone!

Don't let the opinion of others get in the way of *you* creating the business you want. As you grow as a business owner you'll rely more and more on yourself and care less about the opinions of others.

Getting Past Excuses and Moving Out of Your Comfort Zone

> Whatever scares you, go do it, because then it won't scare you anymore. With almost anything, once you do it, it's not as scary as you thought it was.
>
> —DEREK SIVERS

If you are terrified of public speaking and decide to do public speaking every day for six months, do you think at the end of that six months you would be as scared? When the unknown becomes known, it's a lot less scary.

Logically you can accept that. I'm sure that part makes sense. But how can you make yourself go into the unknown, when every piece of you doesn't want to?

Or even before that, what happens if you don't even realize your unconscious mind is stopping you?

Millionaires and Their No-Excuses Approach

> People reject something they fear or don't understand. What I have learned is to take away people's excuses or let them give you any excuse, because I found out that if it's an excuse, any excuse will do. In other words, they're just looking for a reason to validate why they don't want to do anything.
>
> —BRIG HART, NETWORK MARKETER
> AND FOUNDER, R3GLOBAL

Before we get into the *how* to leap into the unknown and face your fears we have to uncover hidden fears.

The *Cambridge Dictionary of American English* says:

> Make Excuses: To give false reasons why you cannot do something.

I'm not saying millionaires don't have excuses. They do. I do, too!

One way our brains try to circumvent the fear is to avoid it. Make excuses. Have you ever caught yourself in an excuse? I think this is one of the first ways we can recognize and start to move past our fear and confidence issues.

Be honest with yourself, because if you don't know it's an excuse you will think it's true! Be aware. It can be really easy to hear excuses from other people but hard to notice them when they come out of your mouth.

Action Item

Ask a trusted friend to call you out and give you honest, tough-love feedback and constructive criticism on your presence or work habits. Or have a mentor or fellow business owner call you out. This part might be painful to hear, but it will be one of the fastest ways to get you to notice them. (I know from experience!)

Here are a few of the most common excuses.

Excuse #1: "I Don't Have Any Time!"

Your management of time will dictate your velocity of success.
—RAY HIGDON, RAYHIGDON.COM

I was talking with a millionaire the other day about how entrepreneurs want the newest tips and tricks to give them more time. In reality, though, it's the fundamental elements that matter. The word *focus* has come up hundreds of times in the 100 interviews. We all have the same amount of time. Imagine if you removed everything from your schedule tomorrow. No work, no driving, no eating, no Facebook, no Twitter, no cat videos, no random surfing, no reading blogs, no reading books, no TV. Just sitting. How long would tomorrow feel? In business, we dilute our efforts by adding so much to our plates.

Len Schwartz, founder of Pro2Pro Network, said:

> It became incredibly obvious to me that I was diluting myself and my efforts and my focus and my energy so much so that I was just spinning plates and getting nowhere. So, for all of you listening that are like that and/or have experienced that, please embrace the value of extreme focus.

Many successful businesses were built in just a few hours a week. Take David Heinemeier Hansson from 37signals. He said, "So on the programming side of things, for about six calendar months that we worked on Base Camp, I spent 10 hours per week. That's it." In a job, it's about how many hours you work. But for an entrepreneur that's not it at all. It doesn't matter how many hours you work. It matters what you produce in those hours.

Michael Burcham, serial entrepreneur who runs the Nashville Entrepreneur Center, said:

> Entrepreneurs aren't rewarded necessarily by effort or hours. We're rewarded when the outcome, the product or service we're producing, actually does something that people care about. I see all the time individuals who are totally putting in crazy hours.
>
> The things they are spending their time on are so unimportant. I mean they're refining page 21 of a business plan describing an operating model in an area form that no one is ever going to read. That's a complete waste of energy. So I would submit to you that it's much more about what constructively you are doing every day and less about how long you are doing it for.
>
> I mean, my own personal philosophy is I give everything a really good 6 to 10 hours in a day.

Action Item

Take at least 30 to 60 minutes today to figure out what you are focusing on. Is everything on your plate truly moving you forward toward what you want? What is the one goal you want to focus on or accomplish this year?

(Stay tuned for Chapter 9 for more information on figuring this out!)

Excuse #2: "I Don't Have Enough Money!"

> You can make excuses or you can make money but you can't do both.
>
> —PAT MESITI

Money is always an issue for a newer entrepreneur, whether you have some or you don't. This is one of the most common excuses I hear from prospects and clients, but **money is not your issue**. Your creativity and pushing through boundaries is the issue. Don't get me wrong—it might be true that you have very little money to spend, but many of the millionaires have had the same issues.

MJ Demarco, author of *The Millionaire Fastlane*, said:

> For someone to say "Oh, I don't have any money. How am I going to start a business?" That's an excuse. It really is. I started my business with $900. All the capital that came into my business was human capital. Hard work, sweat, and the other thing I want to mention is that it was all self-taught. I was on the Internet, learning and buying books; I was at the library all the time.

Joy Gendusa from PostcardMania.com said:

> When I started doing postcard marketing for my company I had no money. So it was literally my paycheck that was going into postage and I started out sending 1,000 pieces every single week.

They find a way. I've heard stories of going to SCORE (Service Corps of Retired Professionals, a free service to help you with your business), figuring out how to get people to work for you for free or for trades, or learning how to do things yourself. In fact, the time we live in now is probably the cheapest to start a business. We no longer have to have a brick-and-mortar store. We no longer have to pay for expensive printed brochures, or telephone book advertisements. Now we have free blogging platforms, social media sites like Fiverr.com, forums, and more. Instead of thinking how little you have, start to think about how much you have.

David Heinemeier Hansson also said:

> It has never been easier to create something in software with no capital on hand as it is today. If you can do it self-funded, you can do it on your schedule, on your own time and with you being in control of the entire process the entire way.

(And a side note about funding: You don't need to get funding. In fact, most of the millionaires I asked said they discourage it. Most of them didn't even take loans, especially in online businesses. They started small, and just kept working and reinvesting. In the survey I asked, "Did you get funding or bootstrap?" Ninety-three percent said they bootstrapped their first business.)

Action Item

Figure out how much money you really do have to invest. Then write all the things down that you would like to be able to do in your business. Then go research to see if you can get the same results you want for a lot cheaper.

Excuse #3: "I don't know how!"

You may not know who, but other people have been there before and succeeded. Just because you don't know how right now, does not mean you can't learn. Sometimes you even paralyze yourself because you don't want to make a wrong move, or you think we need to learn the "right" way. (There isn't a "right" way, so you keep looking continuously.) This excuse is usually based in fear—fear of the unknown and fear of failure. Fear is normal though, for you and for millionaires. They feel it and proceed anyway.

Frank McKinney didn't know how to do real estate before he started, just like Craig Wolfe didn't know how to make rubber ducks that look like celebrities called CelebriDucks. If we already knew how to do every step it probably wouldn't even be that interesting to us. The only thing you need to know is the next step. Figure out what that next step is. If you don't know, ask someone who does.

Action Item

Just take a single action on your next step toward becoming an eventual millionaire, and for now, let go of what might happen after that step. Just start moving forward. Once you make it a habit to recognize your excuses and see them as small hurdles to overcome, you will move forward. You can start to laugh at the silly excuses your brain comes up with to stop you from moving out of your comfort zone. What is more important: excuses or living the life you want?

Moving Past Your Fear

Excuses are one part of the puzzle. When you can start to learn and recognize your excuses you can start to move past them. Most of the time excuses are a mask that covers up the fear. Once you remove the excuse, your fear starts to show through and you can address it.

I've outlined a step-by-step process to help you move past your fear, along with specific tools you can use to help harness it. The first step is to recognize the fear. Goal number one of your new plan about getting uncomfortable every day, recognize the fear. Number two is harness that fear. Number three is step out with active actions and number four is assess and expand your comfort zone. Let's step into those.

Step 1: Recognize the Fear

We tend to avoid things that we don't like and procrastinate whatever it is. If, every time you think of public speaking or deciding on a business decision, you start to feel anxiety or that queasy stomach or worry "What if?", then you are starting to deal with fear. Nobody thinks the feeling of fear is fun. We need to know though that it's there and we need to give it a name because then it can start to get smaller.

Fear is an idea in your head. You can say to yourself, "That's just the fear talking! That's not me. Those thoughts are not necessarily true. I'm just scared."

A situation in your head might go something like this: A mentor suggests that you start public speaking as a way to get more business.

The thoughts in your head go like this:

I don't think that would really help.
I'm not sure if all of that effort is worth the trouble.
I've never been good at public speaking.
There is so much competition for that around here! It would be too hard to break into.
I don't have enough time for that!

I'm not saying that some of these might not be somewhat valid. But our brains automatically come up with some reason to not do something when we are scared. It's almost a knee-jerk reaction. It doesn't really matter if it's true or not, as long as it prevents the fear.

Recognize that it's not really about the competition, or the work, or if you are good at first (none of us are good at first!), but it's truly about you being afraid of it. It's okay to have fear. You need to be aware that it's the fear talking and not what might be best for you.

You need to know where that comfort zone is before you can step out of it.

Action Item

Write down what truly scares you. You don't have to show it to anyone, in fact, you can burn it. But it needs to be brought into the light. If you can't even pinpoint it, you don't know what you are dealing with.

An imagination is a powerful thing. If you are in a pitch black cave and hear a scratching noise but don't know what is causing it, your mind will most likely go to a scary place. It automatically thinks worst case. But what if it's a little mouse? Shining a flashlight on your fears will help you understand how to move past them.

Step 2: Harness the Fear

We have nothing to fear but fear itself.
—THEODORE ROOSEVELT

There is a benefit to fear. Millionaires talk about harnessing it. Just like harnessing the wind or water for electricity, we channel fear into something greater. Fear is an indicator as to whether there might be a threat or risk. So use fear as your guidepost. You probably don't look at that picture because that's probably not a good guidepost right now. It looks like it's going to fall apart. But that's where fear is the asset. Just like Chris said, "It might be your gut telling you to stop moving forward because there's potential disaster ahead. You do that check in, and then you do your due diligence. You use it for what it is and then ignore, if it's not true."

The other way that you can harness the fear is to use fear to get over stuff, to move things faster. Use it like you would caffeine. Pretend fear is like your morning coffee getting you buzzed and ready to go for action. The more situations you are in that are fear-inducing (not paralyzing fear where you can't move, but regulated fear) the more you are stepping out of your comfort zone and the more you are going to be able to create the life you want. It's a good thing, not a bad thing.

Did you know that there is power in fear? Most of the time it seems like fear takes away your power. But there is a hidden power in fear that you need to uncover.

You don't want to be fearless. You want to harness the fear and use it for good. Whether it's for building a successful business or living the life you've been afraid to live, your life is more important than the fear!

Fear is like a wall. And if you can learn to climb, you can stay ahead of others. They are stopped by it, but you, you use it to power you up to keep going forward.

When you feel that fear, recheck the plan, and power through it:

You are still on the journey when others quit.
You are still learning and growing when others stay stagnant.
You have the courage to live the life you choose.

If you let fear stop you, it will, every single time. Right now is where you rise up and stop letting it control you. *You* are in control.

Learn the skill of harnessing your fear, not running from it, and look down from the wall you climbed to the others that let fear stop them.

There is a great quote about martial arts that I love:

A black belt is not fearless. A black belt harnesses the power of fear to break through barriers, mental and physical, to persevere when others would succumb to the fear and help others harness the fear as well. Becoming a black belt is not a physical challenge. It's a journey to an even more awakening of one's abilities, characteristics, strengths, weaknesses and purpose. The black belt that we wear is a symbol of our desire to persevere when it would be easier to quit. To stand for what is right and just with peace as our goal, to seek balance in our lives and guide others to find it as well. A black belt does not have superhuman strength; they have simply unlocked the secrets to human's super strengths.

—Unknown Author

Step 3: Active Actions—Expanding Your Comfort Zone

When fear knocks, answer the door. No matter who you think you are, you can become better and if you want something, you get better and go after it. It really boils down to you need to look in the mirror and say I'm the only thing that's holding me back. It's the guy in the mirror that's holding me back, not my friends, not people who say I don't have what it takes, not people who say I don't have the education. It's me.

—Jim Bellacera, Successful Thinkers Network

I asked Jim, a speaker and business owner who created Successful Thinkers Network—a national networking group that brings together success-minded people not only at local events but online as well—how to overcome fear, because it's good to look at yourself in the mirror and say, "Okay, it's me." But then what do we do?

He said, "Just do it. Nike has that saying, 'Just do it.' Even when I was afraid, I did it anyway and I stuck in that momentum. Some people, they are afraid of those mistakes because they don't want to look bad. I look bad all the time but I got better all the time, too. When I walked away from some of my meetings, I would say 'Why did I say that?' but I was able to reflect on those things that went wrong and those became lessons for me."

We know this stuff, right? You've heard some of this before. I know you have, but it's really about ingraining it in your brain. You need to hear it over and over and over again. Then we need to start taking action.

Tim Hamilton, Owner, Astonished Design: Story

I'll tell you a story. When I was in fifth grade, it was right after my family had immigrated from South Africa to Houston. I was 11 or 12 years old. We were at the neighborhood swimming pool and there were a couple different levels of diving boards. The highest level of the diving board was like a story high—8 or 9 feet—and I would sit at that pool in the summer watching my friends and peers jump off that diving board over and over and over again and I at one point had climbed up the ladder and I'd gotten to the edge and I looked down and I just couldn't imagine how they were doing this.

With my tail between my legs, I retreated and climbed back down the ladder. I was just not going to jump off that diving board and obviously that was humiliating. I knew there was something that these kids were getting, they were understanding that I wasn't getting and I would look up at them and watch them dive over and over and over again and eventually the thought popped into my head and I'm glad it did. It's these kids are doing this and they're bobbing back up to the surface and they're pulling themselves out of the water. They're not dying. But that was the fear that I felt when I was at the edge is that by doing this I would do. It was so against my instinct that it felt like I was going to die.

With that information I worked on like installing it as you would software into a computer. I installed that into my brain that other people have done this before me and they didn't die. So I climbed the ladder and I got to the edge and I felt the fear and I felt like I was going to die and I decided that in order to do this I had to just minimize it down to a musculoskeletal set of instructions. I had to get my brain to give my legs instructions to just walk off. That's what it became.

I just decided to step off and so while that was a story from when I was 11 or 12 years old, it's one that I use still today to think about pushing through the fear is that people have done this. Many people have written books about how to build businesses—Michael Gerber and his book *The E-Myth Revisited*. There was a lot of really great books about the tactical steps of business development like I did there walking off the diving board. There are many how-to's. So the big turning point for me was when I just decided to install that decision into my brain that I was going to take the first step from all these books of advice and just start building it. For me, it was actually hiring an employee.

Step 4: Assess and Expand Your Comfort Zone

So what does your comfort zone look like?

As shown in Figure 3.1, the middle is your comfort zone. It's nice and comfy there. Stepping out of that place means you become uncomfortable. There is a distinction between your comfort zone and discomfort zone. It's not all or nothing, you are comfortable or you are going to die. It's good to have some level of discomfort. But it's not good to go into the danger zone.

You step out of your comfort zone, you start to feel uncomfortable. But then there's another piece, right, that's really kind of uncomfortable where you could grow that comfort zone. You start to grow it. But then there's the piece on the very, very outside that's dangerous and I don't want you to be taking those risks. We do want to push the boundaries of our comfort zone but way too much risk is like jumping in with the tiger and thinking that that's a good idea! We don't want to do that.

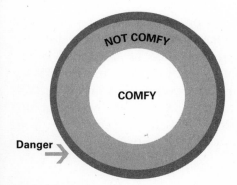

Figure 3.1   Comfort Zone

Your comfort zone can grow. You start to build up a tolerance and then it starts to become comfortable. When I first started doing the millionaire interviews, it was nerve-wracking. My heart started racing a little bit faster, especially at the first millionaire interview. I thought to myself, "Don't look like an idiot!" which made me more nervous!

But now I don't freak out about them at all. It's only relaxing and fun. I can see that my comfort zone has grown. I have to continually step out of my comfort zone, my comfort zone is getting bigger, but I still have to push it so I can grow even more.

Passive versus Active Actions

I like to distinguish between actions—passive actions versus active actions.

Passive actions are actions where you sit in your comfort zone. It's the stuff that's really easy to do like updating something on your website, if you're a tech geek like me, or checking Facebook or accounting or something that is passive. It doesn't get you out of your comfort zone. Don't get me wrong, some of those items are important to your business but it's not making you grow. It's not making you push the boundaries.

Active actions on the other hand are those things that you don't really want to do but you know they would be great for your business. That means stepping out and risking something, either someone saying no or you looking dumb, things like cold calling, sales appointments, or things that you feel anxious about.

I want you to commit to creating a list, things you know you need to do, but that haven't been a top priority, whether it's because you're scared of them or you feel like you have other things going on. Grab that piece of paper and come up with at least three right now. Three things you know you should be doing. We have so much information. We are not starved of information at all.

You know so much already. What are those things that you know you should be doing that you either haven't yet or you haven't done enough of?

Here is a list of ideas:

- Contact a mentor I admire.
- Send my agent my current stories.
- Going to get networking events and pushing myself to talk to more people.
- Put on a seminar.
- Start sending more contact letters.
- Finish a screenplay.

I love this quote from Dan Martell, founder of Clarity.fm:

> Just f'n do it! That is my . . . that's the way I live! If it's a good idea, you do it today! Too many people like think about all the reasons why it shouldn't work or it's too hard or I can't. I think just because I'm so now-focused, my ignorance is bliss. It's like, I don't even think about I can't do it—I just do it and I'm like, "Oh sh**! That's really hard!" I do it anyway.

He even has a license plate that reads JFDI.

Action Item

Commit to getting out of your comfort zone every day.
Do this by creating a list of Active Actions.

Active Actions

_____
_____
_____
_____
_____
_____
_____
_____
_____

Tools to Get Past Your Fear

What if you want to take more active actions but the fear still holds you back? Here are a few tools to help you get past your fear. Not every single one of these are really going to fit for what you're doing. Just think of one action that you want to do this week, and then see if any of these tools will help you get past your fear and do it anyway. Then when you are feeling fear, refer back to these tools and use another one!

Accept the Fear and Let It Pass

Be okay with a sensation of fear. What does it feel like? Bring up something that scares you. If it's public speaking, imagine you're waiting in the wings ready to be introduced and there's 200 people sitting there waiting for you. They are going to judge your appearance as soon as you walk on stage. You might forget everything that you need to say. Try and visualize being there. Take a minute and close your eyes to imagine it. Are you sweating yet?

You'll start to notice the sensations of fear. Your heart starts to pound maybe a little bit faster. Maybe you start to sweat a little bit. Maybe you feel a little queasy in your stomach. These are real physical feelings. They are the sensations of fear. I want you to be able to feel the sensations of fear and sit with them. Don't run from them.

The more you don't want the emotional state, the more it comes up. So when you bring it to the surface, it goes away faster. Don't push it down. Don't try and get rid of it as soon as you can. It's just a feeling. As humans we give a lot of weight to the way we feel. But it's only a feeling.

Instead of thinking that a racing heart means something bad, think of it as something exhilarating. Those same sensations of fear can be familiar and okay in other instances.

Faster heartbeat? That happens when you are in love, or when you are exercising!

Sweating? It's normal! On a 100-degree day are we running from it? If there is no AC in sight, we have to accept it!

Queasy stomach? Most pregnant woman have had to deal with this for weeks straight!

Exercise, a hot day in the sun, and pregnancy are all wonderful things. Our associations with these same sensations are different.

We need to start recognizing fear as a positive, that every time you step out of your comfort zone, it's growing you as a person.

Reappraisal

Reappraisal is visualizing a situation as a neutral person who has the capabilities to handle the situation. Think of that same fearful situation you thought of earlier. Now choose your ideal mentor. Pick a millionaire from this book if you like.

Now pretend you are a millionaire. How would you react to that situation? Your mind-set is bigger. Your comfort zone is bigger.

If you imagined the fearful situation of going out on stage in front of 200 people, and then imagined yourself as Hugh Culver, a millionaire speaker whom I've interviewed, how terrified do you think he would be?

It's all perspective.

Did thinking about that change the way you feel?

So the next time you have an opportunity to expand your comfort zone, try this. Sit back and close your eyes. Imagine the situation you will be experiencing. Then imagine being your mentor. How would they handle the situation? What would they do? If a problem arose, how would they handle it?

Cognitive reappraisal is used by many psychologists to help patients get over trauma or stressful situations or events. The American Psychological Association published a study from Stanford using many different cognitive reappraisal tactics. The tactic we used was named *Agency,* which specifically mentions thinking of a person with skills to change the current situation.

Examples are: Someone will change things, the person has the ability to change, this person can handle the situation, this person has special skills to deal with the situation, the person is being helped by professionals. Note that a person should be specifically mentioned to get a strong agency score.

It was one of the top three tactics for decreasing negativity toward a situation.

Commit in Advance

Let's say you want to grow your business, and know that public speaking or even cold calling would help. Most people (and many clients of mine!) come up with a million excuses not to head down that route. Instead, don't let the excuses stop you, but make the commitment far enough away that you don't need to sweat about it right now.

This technique helps your brain (which is full of excuses) know that it's not in any immediate danger, and still allows you to do the things you want to do—and the event will be booked and much harder for you to get out of later!

So book a speaking gig in four months. It's not scary because it's so far away. Or create the list to cold call, but don't do it until next week. (When next week comes, just set a time limit of only 10 minutes at first to make as many calls as you can!)

I used this same tactic when I decided to launch my podcast. It seemed technically overwhelming at first. So the first action I took was to find and ask a millionaire. Then when one said yes, I scheduled them six weeks out, so I *had* to figure out the technical stuff because I had that looming date. All it took was a simple e-mail, but it stopped all excuses I had!

Worst-Case Scenario

The next technique is worst-case scenario. It's a tactic I've used. It's where you write down the worst things that could go wrong and you figure out how probable they might be. Usually, it's less than 1 percent and only if 17 other things go wrong first. Next, you work out solutions to those problems. It will help you ease your mind. Just know it's really doing it the right way, making sure that you accept the fear and do it anyway; "I know I will still be living after this. What's the worst that can happen?"

A lot of excuses come down to fear: fear of failure, fear of admitting you were wrong, and so on.

So what is the fear? Frank McKinney, a real estate developer (creating $30 million dream homes), said:

> Realize there is a force at work subconsciously in your mind that is tempting you to say no. That's the primary difference between my career and most others especially in real estate, is that I don't let the fear that is there stop me. I do not let it stop me. That is the primary difference.

Put Things in Perspective

I want to take you on a little journey to help you put things in perspective. I have found that doing this really helps put fear in perspective.

Think about yourself. How tall are you? Now think about your fears. They reside in your body and brain.

Now imagine yourself standing next to a three-story building. You are pretty small comparatively.

Now imagine yourself next to Mount Everest. Your fears seem a lot smaller.

Now pan out even more. Imagine you are looking at the Earth (see Figure 3.2). You are a speck that can barely be seen. Your fears are even smaller.

The sun is about 1 million times the size of the Earth. Imagine how small you are in relation to the sun. Now you aren't even a speck.

Now pan back even more. Our sun is one of the smaller suns in our galaxy! The biggest one is more than 1,900 times the size of our sun. And this scenario can go on and on, because our galaxy is so huge many of us can't even comprehend how big.

So, putting things in perspective, we are so small it is ridiculous. Your fear is even smaller than that! Please know that no matter

Figure 3.2   Put Things in Perspective

what happens in the scope of the universe, none of this matters, and the time will pass whether you are doing everything you want in life or not. To me, this is a really good way to get your fears in perspective.

Action Item

Choose one Action to commit to the next time you are feeling fear. Use these tools to manage the fear. Test them and find out which tool works best for you!

Action Tips to Get Past Your Fear and Move Out of Your Comfort Zone

- Accept It
- Reappraisal
- Commit in advance
- Worst-case scenario
- Put things in perspective

What If You Let It Stop You?

Where will you be in five years if you let your fear stop you? Where will you be if you don't?

I know it's easier said than done. But all of these tactics and tools are to get you to take action so you can live the life you want. So you don't become ruled by that small part of your brain that is scared of everything.

Bronnie Ware wrote an article in the *Huffington Post* titled "Top 5 Regrets of the Dying." She had asked hospice workers what the most common regrets were when patients were on their death bed, and the most common regret was, "I wish I had the courage to live a life true to myself, not the life others expected of me."

When people realize that their lives are almost over and look back clearly on them, it's easy to see how many dreams have gone unfulfilled. Most people had not even honored half of their dreams and had to die knowing that it was due to the choices they made or not made. It's very important to try and honor at least some of your dreams long the way. From the moment that you lose your health, it is too late. Health brings freedom very few realize until they no longer have it.

Right now, you're alive and healthy. This is where you make that decision to not let the fear stop you. So that way, when you are in that position and looking back on your life, it's not about what you didn't do or could have done. It's about being okay with what you did, even if that's failing. Strive to overcome any fears, excuses, or lack of confidence you may have and commit and start taking some actions.

Everyone, including millionaires, had to start somewhere, and they did it one action at a time, one thing at a time. Live a life of choices that you want to make, not the ones *you* had to make.

Today is your day to start!

ACTION ITEM REVIEW

Action Item

Ask a trusted friend to call you out and give you honest, tough-love feedback and constructive criticism on your presence or work habits. Or have a mentor or fellow business owner call you out. This part might be painful to hear, but it will be one of the fastest ways to get you to notice them. (I know from experience!)

Action Item

Take at least 30 to 60 minutes today to figure out what you are focusing on. Is everything on your plate truly moving you forward to what you want? What is the one goal you want to focus on or accomplish this year?

Action Item

Figure out how much money you really do have to invest. Then write all the things down that you would like to be able to do in your business. Then go research to see if you can get the same results you want for a lot cheaper.

Action Item

Just take a single action on your next step toward becoming an eventual millionaire, and for now, let go of what might happen after that step. Just start moving forward. Once you make it a habit to recognize your excuses and see them as small hurdles to overcome, you will move forward. You can start to laugh at the silly excuses your brain comes up with to stop you from moving out of your comfort zone. What is more important: excuses or living the life you want?

Action Item

Write down what truly scares you. You don't have to show it to anyone, in fact, you can burn it. But it needs to be brought into the light. If you can't even pinpoint it, you don't know what you are dealing with.

An imagination is a powerful thing. If you are in a pitch black cave, and hear a scratching noise but don't know what is causing it, your mind will most likely go to a scary place. It automatically thinks worst case. But what if it's a little mouse? Shining a flashlight on your fears will help you understand how to move past them.

Action Item

Commit to getting out of your comfort zone every day.
Do this by creating a list of Active Actions.

Active Actions

_____
_____
_____
_____
_____
_____
_____
_____
_____
_____

Action Item

Choose one Action to commit to the next time you are feeling fear. Use these tools to manage the fear. Test them and find out which tool works best for you!

Action Tips to Get Past Your Fear and Move Out of Your Comfort Zone

- Accept it
- Reappraisal
- Commit in advance
- Worst-case scenario
- Put things in perspective

CHAPTER

Finding and Evaluating Your Ideas for Your New Business

The way to get good ideas is to get lots of ideas and throw the bad ones away.

—Linus Pauling

Because one of your goals is to live life on *your* own terms, this chapter seems inevitable! Plus the data shows that the majority of millionaires created their wealth with their own business.

Now the question is, "Have you ever thought of owning your own business?"

I went into the corporate world because I thought that was how it was supposed to be done. I didn't know there was another option. I didn't even realize that I was capable of so much more! It seemed so foreign to me. But now I wouldn't have it any other way.

When you own your own business you control your own destiny, you control the work/life balance, and you take the risk but also reap the rewards. One of the best parts of owning my own business is the people. Now I can choose to only do business with people I consider friends. My work and my personal life have merged in the best way possible.

Many people who have come to me from corporate jobs have the itch. They know there is something more out there, and they have this itch that they don't know how to scratch. They might have business ideas already, but they don't know what will actually work because they have never done it before!

You might be thinking the same thing. I've never done this, it seems so foreign. How do I know what is right?

But you already read the chapter on fear and you know you can get past the feelings of fear. Now you just need to know the "how" part. Keep reading. I want to show you how millionaires found their business ideas, and how they started.

Go through this chapter step by step, and by the end, you should have the idea you can start moving forward on!

How Millionaires Found Their Ideas

The stories I have heard during my interviews has been incredible! The start of each business is always a bit different. However, there are three themes that I want to share.

After going through the data, surprisingly, you'll find that most millionaires did not start their businesses by looking at their passions and creating businesses out of them. That doesn't mean that they don't love or enjoy what they do, however. My research indicates that there are three ways they found their business ideas:

1. **They already had a skill, were working for another company, but decided to venture out on their own.**
    Vonda White: Collegiate Risk Management
    Vonda was one of the top sales professionals at her job, but they seemed to only care about the revenue she produced and not about her fulfillment as a person or a mom who needed some time with her kids. She quit and started her own business. It became a big success, and she has even won the Wachovia Woman Business Owner award.

    Jerry Mills: B2B CFO
    Jerry was a CFO at a company. He saw many professionals getting laid off from their jobs after age 50, and he didn't want that to happen to him. He wanted to take control of his future before that. He started his business when he was 37, but he wasn't any good at sales because he had never learned it. He took a path of learning, and figured

out a method to sell. Now, 10 years later, his company has 210 professionals in 40 different states. They have grown substantially, with revenues around $25 million.

Scott Skinger: TrainSignal

Scott trained people to help them pass computer certification exams. He knew he was pretty good at what he did, but he knew he couldn't leverage the time and effort he was putting in. So he started his own online training company that gave him the reward for his effort and skill.

Marissa Levin: Information Experts

Marissa worked for a company that does information design for the government. She was getting an MBA and knew she was becoming more valuable to the company, so she asked for a raise. Her boss told her that she would never get paid more than $34,000 a year. She already had the skills and so she decided to start her own company. Now her company is doing $17 million of business a year.

2. **Millionaires saw a need in their own lives.**

    ### Sue Ismiel (Nadine): Nad's

    Sue was a medical records keeper in Australia. She had three daughters and all were blessed with her thick, long hair. The problem was they also had thick, long hair on their arms. To help her daughters, she created a product that removed unwanted hair without harsh chemicals and smells. The result was Nad's, an international sensation with infomercials all over the world.

    ### Adam Mesh (Average Joe): Investing Information

    Adam Mesh had done very well as a day trader, but when he went on the reality show *Average Joe*, he was inundated with requests from people to teach him his strategies. He now has a successful business teaching others how to day trade.

3. **They asked people what they needed!**

    ### Dustin Wells: Headspring

    Dustin had an award-winning business plan that failed miserably. He even pivoted and tried a new approach, but that also failed. Eventually he asked businesses what they needed and from the feedback he created his company Headspring, which creates software for companies.

Dane Maxwell: Paperless Pipeline

Dane first created an intranet for real-estate brokers, because he thought that's what they wanted. It turns out, they didn't really need that. Instead of just moving forward, Dane started asking them what they did need. They said they needed a better product than what was in the current market for going paperless. Dane just created what they needed.

How to Generate Business Ideas

> All achievements, all earned riches, have their beginning in an idea.
>
> —Napoleon Hill

It's time to get excited! Now you get to start with your ideas. Everyone has ideas, now is the time to let them lose! As soon as you start to have one or two, once you learn how to look and go with the flow, soon enough you will have dozens. Dozens of opportunities to evaluate.

What I want for you in this is to have fun with it! This process should be fun. Don't put pressure on yourself to find the perfect idea, or the *right* thing. Being open, looking around to see what problems you can help people with is the best way.

That's all that a good business is. A good business is something that solves a problem for someone that needs it solved. The value to the end customer is enough that they want to pay for it. You are helping people solve problems! It's the best job in the world.

You probably already have a few ideas percolating in your brain. I'll go over a structure that will help you generate many more, and then refine them to find out which might be best for *you*.

The "Find Your Passion" Myth

Before we jump into evaluating your business ideas, I want to dispel the "Find Your Passion" myth.

The best ideas come from a *need*, not from your passion.

The best attempt is to match your *skills* (not passion) with a *need* in the market. In business we are told: Follow your passion! There is a market for everything! But there isn't. And when I researched all of the interviewees—*rarely* did they start with what they were passionate about and move forward to create an amazing business.

It is a lot of pressure to think that you have to find your sole purpose in life, pursue it, and be successful. To look for that one thing, to find the magic key to success is incredibly crippling.

I know because I felt that way! I was trying to answer the question of what is my life's purpose with this one idea. But there isn't just one door. There are *many* doors that will lead to an amazing life.

So please please please put your mind at ease.

Anything you choose will have pluses and minuses. There will be pieces of your business that you adore. There will be pieces that are not fun. This is especially true when you are first starting and are trying to do too much yourself. Your journey will have many twists and turns. As you step through that one door, many other possibilities will open up that couldn't be seen beforehand.

Cal Newport, author of *So Good They Can't Ignore You: Why Skills Trump Passion in the Quest for Work You Love,* and researcher at Georgetown, talks about careers in this instance, but the research works for business, too.

He says:

- People who end up loving their work rarely have definite pre-existing passions.
- Don't seek the perfect job, seek to get more positive traits in the job you already have.
- Don't set out to discover passion, set out to develop it.

> I've watched too many of my peers fall into anxiety and chronic job-hopping due to this flawed advice. The issue is expectations. If you believe that we all have a pre-existing passion, and that matching this to a job will lead to instant workplace bliss, then reality will always pale in comparison.
>
> Work is hard. Not every day is fun. Building the skills that ultimately lead to a compelling career can take years of effort. If you're seeking a dream job, you'll end up disappointed, again and again.
>
> —CAL NEWPORT

I see a lot of this type of thinking when people are starting a business.

This is the mentality:

> "I'm going to try this thing . . . Dabble a bit and see if it takes off. See if I like it. See if it's the right fit."
> Time passes . . .
> "Well, that really isn't what I want. Let's try this idea. This one is *great!*"

I know this happens, because this is *exactly* what I did. I had many misconceptions of business. Here are a few of the things I tried within three months:

- Created a product idea and prototype and submitted a provisional patent.
- Created an iPhone app.
- Started a blog to see what blogging was all about (EventualMillionaire.com).
- Created more business ideas than I knew what to do with.

None of them "took off." After weeks of working hard, I was discouraged. I didn't see any progress with any of them. No revenue at all. I kept jumping to a new idea at every road block. I thought it was me. Maybe I wasn't good at this.

As I learned more about business, and how to tell what was a viable idea, I realized that the one key piece that I was missing over and over again was my commitment.

I wasn't willing to climb over the roadblocks. I was under the assumption that a business that worked well should be easier. (For those that knew better, insert laughter here!)

Well, business isn't always *easy* and you won't like all parts of it. I can guarantee that!! *But* the goal behind business is to do what you have to do at first, and then get to a point where you only do the things you enjoy.

One way to commit more is to line up who you are with what you are doing. Your core values need to line up. Otherwise you are just in it for the money. (Which is not what this book is about.) That doesn't mean you have to find your single life's purpose. That does mean that you need to figure out what you care about, as a person. And it's much more broad than you think.

Adii Pienaar, an interviewee who built WooThemes.com from zero to 150,000 paying subscribers in five years, said this:

> You basically need to know what your personal values and characteristics are, and mostly what you're passionate about. I think it's so easy for us, especially these days where anybody can pretty much launch almost any business within industry.
>
> Entrepreneurs would spot opportunities where they believe that this is a big opportunity, and I can make loads of money for example, or I can build a fascinating business around it, but they're not necessarily passionate about it. I think that's kind of the surest way that you can just fail. Right there and then because it's not sustainable.
>
> I think you can probably put up a billion-dollar business with a photo sharing app, but if you're not passionate about it, that's going to be it, you know. Money is going to be your end game. For some people that's fine. If you want to build a lasting sustainable profitable brand, you need to kind of make sure from the very first day those things that you put into your brand actually aligns with who you are as a person.

I think *passion* is a loaded word. We all interpret it a bit differently. "Finding your passion" is something that is thrown around a lot. It sounds like that if I like karate, I should be a karate instructor. Or if I am passionate about a specific hobby I should be doing that. I think we all have many passions. And sometimes hobbies should stay as hobbies! Because as soon as you transfer it into something you *have* to do, things change. But that doesn't mean you can't line up your core values and things that you love with your business ventures.

For example, many people I interview are extremely passionate about giving back. You could start a business that you aren't necessarily hugely passionate on, but make it so that every widget you sell, you give a portion to your favorite charity. That small thing can spark a passion to grow and help more and more.

Please understand that all of this is a process. You aren't going to know exactly what works and doesn't work right now. But we are lucky. In the world we live in right now, we have the capacity to learn and grow for many, many years.

It's a journey and a test.

So before we dig into all of this, and start figuring out ideas and so on, I have to tell you an amazing piece of advice from Derek Sivers, creator of CD Baby, which I refer to often.

Don't Be a Donkey

We have to focus on one business at a time. But what happens if you can't because you are unwilling to pick your focus? We want to do it all, even if the evidence clearly shows the contrary. Have you ever felt this way?

Every time I hear someone talk about this being an issue I bring up this fable, which Derek Sivers, who founded a couple of successful businesses, brought to my attention.

Derek Sivers: There's a parable of a donkey that is exactly equidistant between two buckets of water; one is 30 feet to the left, one is 30 feet to the right. He keeps looking left, looking right, keeps looking at both buckets, can't decide because they both look equally appealing and eventually he falls over and dies of thirst.

The reason the donkey was in that situation or the reason the donkey died of thirst is that donkeys can only see the present moment. They can't future think and say, "Oh well, you know what, I can walk over to that one first and then walk over to the other one next." Donkeys can't think that far ahead. So whenever people are feeling like they're in that situation, it's because they're not thinking far enough ahead. They're living too much in the present moment only and not looking at the long term.

Because if you look at the long term, if you think of yourself as 90 years old looking back at your life, and you think of right now—say you're 25 and you have 10 different things you want to be doing and you think "I can't get anything done." Well, you can actually do them all, it's just that you have to be patient and do them sequentially, like the donkey with the buckets of water. So you have 10 different ideas. Well throw yourself into one for two years. Actually write it down, make a rough draft of a life plan saying, "For the next four years I will do this business and then for the next four years I will throw myself into that and for the next five years then I will go be a mountain climber and then for the next four years then I will start a music school."

With all those different aspirations you have in life, don't be a donkey. Look long term and realize you can do them sequentially if you're patient and then you can do one at a time and throw yourself into it totally. We've all experienced this on a micro level. Say, for example, that feeling you have when it's crunch time. Something is due tomorrow and you absolutely have to do it tonight because it's due in the morning, so you're throwing yourself into it, completely focused on it, and sure you may get tired, you may rub your eyes and you think for a second, "I would like to be snorkeling right now," or whatever it may be.

But you don't go snorkeling now because you know that you need to focus on the task at hand in order to get it done at all. But if you were to stop and go snorkeling right now, nothing would ever get done. I think it can be the same thing, where you zoom out and instead of down to the minute, make that months or years of your life that you have to realize that you won't get anything done at all if you don't focus on one thing. So those other things you want to do like going snorkeling, yes, you will do them, just be patient. You'll do them whether it's in a few months or a few years, you'll do them, but you have to focus on this one thing right now.

The Time Factor

We are so lucky that we can do this! Not too long ago, it was commonplace to get a job and work at it for 40 years. Now you can really do what you want, just not all at the exact same time.

What do you pick to start with? The best answer to that question is with another question. "Which one of these things would be better if I do it now, while I'm younger or while the opportunity is fresh?"

This can bring clarity because some of the items on your list do have a time frame! If there is a specific business you want to build and it's a hot trend right now, maybe in 10 years it won't be.

And don't worry if you aren't 25. The fact is, we are living longer and longer, so whether you are 25 or 55, you have time.

Action Item

Create your life plan:

1. Grab a piece of paper.

Your Life Plan

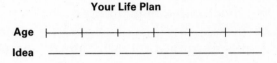

Age

Idea

2. Draw a line in the middle.
3. Write your age at the far left.
4. Write five-year increments.
5. Place one idea in each section.

Look long term and realize that you have time to be patient.

We are all living longer. Keep your health and, barring any freak accidents, you will be able to accomplish so much in your lifetime. Yet we start a business and it has to be the *one* thing we do forever.

We spend four years in college to prep, and we start a business and think everything will go great from the get go.

What if you decided to spend four years failing over and over again at business? You would get a *better* education, and it would probably be cheaper than $35,000 a year for college!

All of this Starts with an Idea

Millionaires don't think ideas are worth much. You've heard that ideas are a dime a dozen. And it's true! Successful people have *way* more ideas then they could *ever* implement. But that doesn't mean you don't need to start with a good idea.

It still is part of the equation. If you have a crappy idea and you are an amazing marketer you can make money at it. *For a short time.*

In the world we live in, with social media and sharing opinions constantly, if the idea/level of the product isn't good, everyone will know. But even if you have an amazing idea, it doesn't matter. You need to build your skill level so you can *really* make the idea achieve what it's capable of. You also need to know how to sell it.

Your first job is to gain the skills. Jumping into business is the best way to actually learn the skills you need to build a successful business. You won't learn it by reading about how others do it. (Not that you shouldn't do that, too! But implementing and learning from others are two very different things.)

Imagine serial entrepreneurs, people who have been successful in the past, taking on a really great idea. They will be able to develop it better and faster than you ever could.

So, the learning curve for you is to learn the business. Use the idea as a tool to *learn* the business as your skill.

Great, so how do I find the idea?

It all starts with brainstorming. I want you to commit to coming up with a ton of ideas. Many of them will suck. You might have only a few good ideas in the mix, but that's okay. Don't judge any of the ideas. You don't know where your bad ideas will lead you. The bad ideas might lead you to your best one yet, so make sure to keep it in the mix.

For now, let's take a week or so of just looking around. Problems are *everywhere*. Commit to writing down problems and ideas as they come up.

 Action Item

Get Your Right Idea in Four Steps

1. List 10 things you already know very well: current job skills, hobbies, and so on.
2. List 10 ideas where you see a need.
3. List 10 industries you might want to work in: ones you're passionate about, want to learn, and so on.
4. Take these lists and ideas, and grab a journal. Start to think about these industries and areas and see if there are any opportunities to solve a problem. Start talking to others in the industry and see if you can come up with your business idea. Write down a list of at least 10 problems that you can solve.

This step may take some time. That's okay, but give yourself a deadline on when you will need it complete by. Try about a week. Otherwise you will never actually pick an idea.

Finding problems to solve becomes easier as you tune into it more. Ideas can come out of the blue. So make sure you have that journal with you everywhere. (Or use your smartphone to keep track of the ideas.) I find the best ideas often come at night, just as I'm trying to go to sleep, or in the morning when I wake up. I also love thinking over ideas in the shower, or when I'm running. I've found the best places are when your body is busy but your mind can be quiet.

This is a process, and if you don't like any of the ideas you have come up with, start asking other people where they see a problem to be solved. I'm sure that will spark many ideas!

How Millionaires Evaluate Ideas

So you have an idea. Loads of people have good ideas, but don't do anything after that step!

You are different, though. You are committed to figuring this out. So the next step is really trying to evaluate what might work and what won't. Now we can't predict the future (it would be a lot easier if we could!) so instead we'll ask a lot of questions to see what seems to fit your lifestyle, your circumstances (start-up costs, competition already out there), and the market.

There are three tests I suggest to evaluate your ideas before you choose one. Grab your list of ideas, you should have many by now. We will methodically go through each one to see what fits best for your life, your wallet, and the market.

1: Lifestyle Test

This includes questions like, "What will my life look like in 2 years, 5 years, 10 years?" Some millionaires didn't understand what commitments, schedules, and requirements were necessary before they started. If your business doesn't fit within your life plan, then you may come to resent it. For example, if your business makes you travel a lot for the first two years but you love being home with your family, then is it the right choice?

Adrian John Cartwood, a personal finance blogger, said,

> What was the end game? The end game for me isn't working and the end game for you isn't working either. We all work and do things to achieve the end game. The end game for me was I wanted to be a traveler and I wanted to travel not just physically but mentally and spiritually and that's very hard to explain to people. I came up with what I call my life's purpose. I found what I wanted to do with my life.
>
> What I really wanted to do was have the freedom to do lots of different things and to expand my mind, expand my philosophies and I realized if you want to do lots of things and travel, you can't very well be tied down to a job or a business 50 or 60 hours a week. It just doesn't work.

Adrian's life purpose wasn't just about work. It was about his *whole* life.

What type of life do you really want? You really only have one life, and we restrict our thinking of what we *should* want. I hear things like, "Well I would love to get out of the 9 to 5 grind but let's be realistic."

Let's be realistic? You know there are people in the world doing *exactly* what you want to be doing. Open yourself up to those possibilities.

When you start to open yourself up to the possibilities, many thoughts might come into your head. Some are happy and daydream-like, possibilities of working from the beach or going to amazing destinations.

But what also tends to crop up are negative thoughts. You may be thinking, "Who am I to get that?" or "I have a family to think about, I can't have it all." Put those thoughts out of your head for now. While we are going through this right now, pretend you are a millionaire already.

You know you can succeed—you just have to figure out the logistics of what you want. So what do you *really* want?

Choosing Money or Lifestyle First   There are many possibilities when it comes to enjoying your life and running your business. You can decide. Here are two that I hear about often.

Working Insanely and Selling for a Big Payout   One option is to work a ridiculous amount upfront, and create a sellable asset, so you can sell the company and cash in on a lot of money all at once. This is what you see a lot in the tech startup community. Fast growth so you can sell. This is definitely a viable option.

MJ Demarco, a millionaire who sold Limos.com, worked ridiculously hard for years and years. He had many failed businesses, but eventually he had a huge payout. He lives life on his own terms. He was able to reap the rewards of all of his hard work.

This option works better when you don't have a family, or prior commitments. It's best when you have really low expenses and expectations, and love working 80-plus hours a week to see something grow.

An Example My good friend Maren Kate was in my mastermind group. Years ago she had a good lifestyle business online. She had a company that did social media marketing, which was all virtual, and a blog and podcast all about creating a lifestyle business.

Then she met MJ Demarco, one of the millionaires I interviewed. His philosophy is to work your butt off for five years and then sell your business for millions and live off the interest. That way, you work ridiculously hard at first, but then have the freedom for the rest of your life to have whatever lifestyle you want.

She ended up leaving that meeting changed. She started looking for the business idea that would be big. It wasn't about just living the lifestyle anymore. It was about creating something that would become a sellable asset.

I watched the process of her figuring out an idea, testing it, pivoting, testing it, pivoting. It was amazing to watch the process.

She now has a company called Zirtual, which provides U.S. -based executive assistants to businesses. Within two years of starting and proving the revenue model, she has 150 employees, and she just took on $2 million of funding from Tony Hsieh of Zappos.

Creating a Lifestyle Business from the Start The other option is to create a business that works *around* your lifestyle. It will likely grow more slowly, but you'll be able to enjoy the lifestyle you want while you are building it.

You live on your terms and don't sacrifice everything for the business. There is a fine line, though, because starting a business does take a lot of time and work! But this option works well for people who are still in a corporate job. It's about making slow and steady progress forward.

An Example   I interviewed Sean Malarkey, who has an amazing business training professionals in social media and business growth. He is a living example of how to run a business around his lifestyle.

He doesn't like having to schedule time in advance, so his type of business doesn't need many specific meeting times. He loves to surf and makes it a point to be surfing whenever he can. He has a beautiful family that he adores spending time with, and has a really cute home office. (Watch Sean's interview and you can see the amazing view from his office balcony, too.)

It was all in the plan. He had a goal and did it all on purpose.

Finding the Lifestyle Fit   Below are a few questions and examples to help you figure out your ideal lifestyle. Let me be clear, you won't know *exactly* what you want until you try many things. You probably know what you don't want right now. But that is only a small slice of what you don't want. It's hard to know exactly what you do want until you do it, and say, "*Yes* this is amazing!"

For right now, all we can do is guess. If you know you hate waking up early in the morning yet decide to start an organic farm raising animals, that might not be a good fit. Or you might decide to be an international speaker and travel 260 days out of the year, but have a family at home and hate to be away that much.

I know this sounds like common sense, but many of us start on a path and don't realize where that path is leading. Before we truly start, I want to make sure that you want to end up at the destination you are pointing at!

This, too, is a process. For now we want to pick something that seems good right now. Don't worry if it's not "perfect." We just need something very clear to aim at—what you think you will like better than where you are now.

Grab your idea list and we will evaluate them based on the lifestyle you want.

What Does Your Ideal Day Look Like?   A great exercise to use is to imagine your perfect day. Don't worry about what you are doing during your work hours right now.

How did you sleep and what time did you wake up?
What is the weather like outside?
How are you feeling? Healthy, excited, calm, stress-free?
What are you going to wear?
What are you having for breakfast?
What does your living space look like?
What part of your day is "work"?
Where do you work? (At home, at your own office?)
Do you like having scheduled appointments to look forward to,
    or do you want to do things spur of the moment?
Who do you spend the day with?
What do you have for lunch?
What is your attitude like?
What are you excited about? (Planning a vacation or trip? Work
    goals?)
Do you log into your bank account? What numbers do you see?
What does the evening look like?
Do you have something planned or is it a relaxing evening in?
What does your bedtime routine look like?
Do you pray or meditate?

Write down what you see as an amazing day.
As an extra bonus, take a look at how your ideal day compares
to the typical day you have now. How far off is it?

Action Item

Write out your ideal day. Be as detailed as possible. Keep it somewhere safe, like in a special journal so you can look back at it.
(I find looking back at it to be *amazing*!)

Action Item: Your Idea List Lifestyle Evaluation

Now it's time to grab that idea list. We want to check through each idea and figure out how it matches up to what your ideal lifestyle is like. There can be a big difference between offline businesses, or owning a physical location, and an online virtual business. These three steps help you figure out what side of things you like best.

1. Write down the ideas on the left.
2. Write down a quick synopsis of what your lifestyle might look like.
3. On a scale of 1 to 10, rate how close this lifestyle comes to your perfect lifestyle.

Idea	Lifestyle Like	Rating
1.		
2.		
3.		
4.		
5.		
6.		
7.		
8.		
9.		
10.		

The rating scale makes it easy to cross off ones that don't fit.

Action Item

1. Cross out any idea that has a rating of less than 7.
2. Fill out the worksheet. You can download the starter kit at http://EventualMillionaire.com/StarterKit.
3. Go through the list of ideas you have and cross out the ones that don't fit with your lifestyle.

2: Circumstances Test

There is always more at play than just having a good idea that fits a market. What also matters is what you have to work with, and what fits your life! These questions will help you start to figure out what business is best for you to start based on how much money you have to start it, what current competitors already exist, what lifestyle you want, and what you are passionate about.

Start-Up Costs Get a rough estimate of what the start-up costs would be for your business idea. This will help you decide on the right idea later. You won't know exactly what these are, so just do a preliminary search. If you are looking to start an organic farm, the costs for land might be substantial. That's what we want to know in advance.

An online business might take a lot less upfront capital. It might only need a website, and a marketing budget. If you are a local service provider, like a web designer, you might just need to pay to go to networking events and sell your services! It really depends on the business you are going into. Right now we are just looking for a general idea of start-up costs so we can pinpoint the best business to start based on the logistics.

Start-Up Expenses

Buildings/real estate/leasing	$
Equipment	
Location/administration expenses	
Opening inventory	
Marketing/advertising expenses	
Other expenses	
Contingency fund	
Total Start-Up Expenses	$

Action Item

Go through and eliminate the business ideas you have that do not fit with your ability to fund the start-up costs.

If you have an amazing idea but the upfront costs are high, that doesn't mean don't do it if you think it's going to be huge. That just means you might need to get creative on funding it. We are so lucky to have websites that are crowd-funding platforms, like kickstarter.com or indiegogo.com. Websites like these not only can provide you with the start-up costs, but also validate your idea! It's one of the best ways to start a new business that needs funding.

SWOT Analysis   By now you should have started to narrow down your list. Ideally, you will only be doing this step for a few of your ideas.

A SWOT analysis (strengths, weaknesses, opportunities, threats) is a tool to really determine what the industry looks like for your start-up business. It will go over your strengths, weaknesses, opportunities, and threats to give you a better picture of what you might be dealing with when you start.

Harvard Business Essentials: Strategy gives a great tool for identifying what's solid about your business plan and what can be improved. Analyze your business idea under these four lenses to determine how you stand.

1. Strengths: Characteristics of the business that give it an advantage over others.
2. Weaknesses: Characteristics that place the business at a disadvantage relative to others.
3. Opportunities: External chances to improve performance in the environment.
4. Threats: External elements in the environment that could cause trouble for the business.

Research Needed   Research at least five of your top competitors. See what they are doing well, and what they aren't doing well. Figure out where your company could fit. Start researching the industry to see where it is going. Is it increasing? Or are a lot of companies going out of business and things declining?

Then start to fill in this template:

Strengths	Weaknesses
Opportunities	Threats

Here's an example:

Strengths	Weaknesses
New concept to the industry Advanced technology	Lack of experience in the industry Little start-up capital
Opportunities	**Threats**
Industry is rapidly growing Big distribution network	Low barriers to entry Competitors have huge market share

Action Item

Create a SWOT analysis for the top three business ideas you have. Delve into the competition that exists so you can see a clear picture of what you are up against.

3: What Does the Market Want: Feedback

Michael Burcham, creator of the Nashville Entrepreneur Center, sums up this section:

> One should always start with some sort of visual picture or flowchart or even a few power point pictures. Show what you are trying to create and then get that in front of three or four trusted advisors to get feedback. Then as soon as you have what feels like a prototype of what this might be, a service or a product, get in front of potential customers and say this is what I'm thinking would solve your pain.
>
> This is how it would look. This is how much it would cost, what it would do if I build this and get it for you, is this something you would do?
>
> Then really start drilling into under what conditions. If you do that back and forth, you can usually have that prototype pretty much ready to go within a month. That second month you can use to refine it based on the feedback you're getting

from customers and in that third month, you pretty much can say okay let's get this into a launch plan.

The importance of feedback is a common theme from millionaires. Brenton Hayden, owner of Renter's Warehouse, said:

> You know if you've gotten enough feedback if your confidence has gone up or down as a result. If you're getting feedback and your confidence is going down in your program, you might not be ready yet.
>
> You can reduce your risk by figuring out what your market wants before you invest a lot of time and money. Neil Patel said, "You don't have to have a finished product or service. You'd be shocked by how many companies out there sell before they actually have their finished product or service. You create a minimal viable product."

The great thing about getting feedback is that not only will you hear what your potential customers say about your idea, you will also get better at explaining it. It will help you solidify what your business is when you talk about it over and over again.

Follow these four steps to get feedback on your business idea:

1. Flowchart or outline.

You need to have something to show your potential customers in order to get feedback. It's easier to have something visual to show potential customers, especially if it's a service or something that hasn't been created yet.

Grab a piece of paper. You can also use mind-mapping software, or even just PowerPoint (or Keynote for Mac). Answer these seven questions:

1. How would your potential customers first interact with your product or service?
2. How would they get more information before their decision?
3. How do they make their decision?
4. How do they pay?
5. How is the value exchanged? How do they receive it?
6. What happens after the exchange?
7. Any last steps?

You should be able to clearly identify three parts of the diagram:

1. Your costs.
2. Where revenue comes in.
3. Where the value experience happens.

Your Costs

This is what you spend your money on. It might be advertising or marketing to get the customer. It might be sales people. You may have costs for the physical good, or the delivery of the service.

Where Revenue Comes In

You need to be able to clearly identify where your revenue is coming in, and who specifically pays you.

Where the Value Experience Happens

When does the customer recognize the value? What type of experience do they have? This is the reason why they would tell others about you.

2. Identify your potential customer.

You need to make sure you can reach your customer. This helps in targeting and lets you know who you need to talk to. Finding your potential customer includes asking these key questions:

- What is their pain?
- What other things do they buy?
- Do you know of anyone who fits the description?

3. Pitch it.

Find 5 to 10 of your potential customers to get in front of. That means calling them or e-mailing and asking to sit down with them individually. Create questions to ask them, and prep a pitch of your idea in case their pain points line up with your idea.

You also want to pitch it to trusted advisors, not just potential customers.

Chris Gravagna, Owner of Wines by Wives, said:

I've always used friends, family and trusted advisors—my network—to get feedback. I verbalize my ideas a lot. I talk to people and people are opinionated. People like to give their opinions—good or bad. I try to find people who usually give me their bad opinions and say, "Oh no that's not going to work."

With my newest business, I went to probably about 100 people and talked about the idea with them. One or two out of that group gave me nothing but negative feedback poking holes in it. That helped me in filling in those holes to make the idea better.

Usually, I'll go with an idea to someone and I'll get a lot more negativity on an idea; "This is what you shouldn't do," or "That's not going to work." With this very specific idea, we had so much positive feedback: "Wow, that's a great idea. I can't believe I didn't think of that one."

The other side, which is always good for us, is "How do I get in? How do I invest?" So I think verbalizing your ideas and going to trusted individuals, mentors, people that you want to be mentors, you have to verbalize and talk about what you want to do. That will help you in getting a little bit more confident or help you in changing or manipulating your idea to make it better and then coming back and saying, "You know what, this is what we changed with the idea."

4. Get their feedback.

Ask your potential customer these questions to get their take on your business idea:

- Under what conditions would you buy it?
- What price would you pay?
- *Make-It-or-Break-It Question:* When can I expect that you and I would sign a letter of intent for that purchase?

This last question is a critical step, especially if you are dealing with consumers and not businesses. Consumers (especially friends and family) will say, "That's a great idea! Yes, I would buy it!" But until they are willing to give you money for it, it doesn't count.

Michael Burcham, a millionaire and CEO of the Nashville Entrepreneur Center, said, "Often I see with early stage companies that there is a pain, and the entrepreneur has designed a product or service to solve the pain, but the potential customers just don't care if the pain is solved or not. They've learned to live with it, and they're not willing to buy a solution. They'll take a free solution." As a new business owner, you need to know if a customer is willing to pay for the solution *before* you invest a lot of money or time!

What about Networking Marketing?

Network marketing is a business model that relies on a network of distributors to grow a business. You may have heard of many different network marketing businesses. Most millionaires suggest starting your own business because you have a lot more control, and you own everything.

However, I have interviewed a few millionaires who made their money in networking marketing, and I just want to give you a short pros and cons list for starting with network marketing.

Pros

- Network marketing is great training for anyone new to business, especially in sales.
- It's a proven product or service and you can get started right away.
- It provides passive recurring income most of the time.

Cons

- You don't own the company and they can take away the compensation or kick you out (this happened to millionaire Brig Hart).
- You have to be fully committed to make it work (just like in any business!).
- Many people look down on network marketing because there are some bad salespeople in the industry.

I would suggest that you do your research and gain feedback in the same way if you are choosing a network marketing company. You want to know if the products are solving a need and useful, and if they will provide the lifestyle that you want to have.

In the end, the most important piece, whether you decide to start with network marketing or your own business, is to commit.

You have got to commit. This is not a 12-hour or 12-day business. You have to commit to being here and doing the same
routine 12 months from now, come hell or high water. There
is going to be health issues, job issues, there are going to be
unexpected costs. They are going to happen. People that are
successful focus on their goals, people that are unsuccessful are
focused on their circumstances.

—RAY HIGDON, NETWORK MARKETER AT RAYHIGDON.COM

Choosing the Right Idea

Value isn't objective. It is subjective on the opinions of others,
not you.

—DEREK SIVERS, CREATOR OF CD BABY

You aren't going to always *know* the best option. Even if you
have a feeling that this will be a hit it might not be!

When I was interviewing Michael Hyatt he mentioned to me his
philosophy on something, which I think aptly applies to this.

I've realized there is no correlation between how I feel about
something I create and what the response is in the market.

—MICHAEL HYATT, AUTHOR

First, realize that you will never have the perfect idea. If you
think it's perfect then, you probably haven't vetted it enough.
There will be obstacles in starting any business. Second, if you are
having a hard time deciding, go with your gut.

Brenton Hayden, CEO of WebDiggs, said this when I asked
him, "Do you ever go by your gut or is it pretty much all nonemo-
tional, what the market wants, that sort of thing?"

Oh yes, my gut has gotten me in a lot of trouble and also got
me a lot of positive benefits and gains. I always go with my gut
feeling. Trust your gut but be smart about it.

Third, realize that you will continually get feedback at all points
in your business. Your job is to determine what to do with that
feedback.

Action Item

Just start the idea that looks the best right now.

There isn't an easy button, even if we wish there were! But the good news is, whether your first business succeeds or fails. You are a success. Whatever happens, the fact that you started is more than most can ever say. Many people have ideas. It's not the idea that counts. It's what you do with it.

So now starts the real journey. You will start on a path that will lead you to a ton of learning. You will become a better person, get past obstacles, learn how to get past your fear, and learn more about yourself than you ever imagined. It all starts with making a decision and taking action to achieve an end result. Even if that end result doesn't happen, it will make you better.

So what do you have to lose?

Product Creation Testing in a Weekend

Start with an industry or target market.
Millionaire Ryan Lee, an Internet marketing expert who holes up in a coffee shop as his office, walked me through choosing something during our interview:

> RL (Ryan Lee): All right, now first thing is it is going to depend on the type of product. I am known in the marketplace to be able to create stuff really, really fast because I get hyperfocused. I'm always distracted but when I am focused I just zoom in. First thing I recommend is you've got to get focused. You've got to put yourself in an environment where you have the ability to just superfocus and not get distracted. So turn off the phone, turn off Skype, and just take that whatever, half an hour, hour, two hours a day, to just work on that first thing in the morning before anything else, before you do e-mail. That's the most important thing.

In terms of product creation, there's different types. What I have done in the past and I recommend and I teach this in one of my systems is if you want to just, it's a little bit more effort but it's a great way to put kind of pressure on yourself and I'll explain it. Let's name another market, Jaime, give me any target market and we'll come up with a kind of a product.

JT (Jaime Tardy):   Can I pick karate?

RL: Let's pick karate. All right, karate. So tell me a little bit more. Are going to teach other people how to become better at karate? Are you going to teach other karate instructors how to open up a karate school?

JT: Actually, let me tell you, I love my karate teachers and what they're actually doing is creating a system for kids, one of the kids has cerebral palsy and so they're teaching actually a whole thing for him and he's doing amazing. What they want to do is sort of replicate that.

RL: So they want to teach other kids with, I worked with so many kids with CP so I used to love working with the kids with cerebral palsy. So they want to sell a system teaching people how to train kids with CP or the actual end user kids with CP?

JT: I think both eventually but yes.

RL: Let's just say it's going to be a product how to train a kid who has cerebral palsy with karate. You're going to sell this to parents and you're also going to sell it to physical therapists, fitness professionals, occupational therapists, whoever. To me, that's a very physical product because you can't do that on PowerPoint. You have to have someone there. You have to be able to demonstrate the exercises and all the different movements. There's got to be video. There has to be a video component.

Here's exactly what I would do if I had that skill set. I would say okay I'm going to make it a one-day workshop. First thing I am going to do is outline. I'm going to sketch out all the components, all the modules. Maybe module one is going to be assessment then maybe we can talk about warm up and dynamic flexibility. Then we can talk about strength training and then we can talk about anaerobic and aerobic conditioning and then we can talk about cool down and then we can talk about programming.

Now each of those I break down. Let's just call them an hour chunk. So 9 A.M. to 10:00 A.M. is going to be the assessment and then you just break it down into those specific chunks. I would then find a space. It's so easy to find space. You can go on Craigslist, you can rent out a gym, you can go into the public library. You can do it in a hotel conference space. You can get it really inexpensively and probably for free, especially if you know anyone who has space—the local YMCA, the local high school, anyone, or you could do it outside. I wouldn't recommend outside for this, though.

Now there's two options, you can either charge for the workshop or you just invite some people for free. So let's say you don't even want to start charging. I would find a couple of people who I know are interested in it. So I would call some local personal trainers and physical therapists and say, "Look I'm going to do this workshop. It's going to be a full day 9 A.M. to 5 P.M. I am going to go through the whole system of how to train a kid with cerebral palsy in karate. It's going to be great. You're going to love it. Come dressed in sweatpants ready to do it." They say, "Okay, great."

Got my space. I would literally, like that's the first thing I am going to do. I am going to get this, before I even have it outlined, I'm getting the space so in two Tuesdays from now I call this space, I get the space, hey in two weeks I'm going to book the workshop 9 A.M. to 5 P.M. Okay, it's $100 deposit, fine, I send the money. Now all of a sudden it's out there.

JT: Deadline.

RL: An external deadline. Now I have no choice. I have to hustle my ass off. I contact the people and then I find the videographer. I go on Craigslist. I look at wedding videographers and I basically give them all the specs. It's going to be this time to this time. Here is the schedule how we're going to film. I'm going to need two cameras. We want good audio. We might need a light kit setup. I am going to need a screen because I am going to do PowerPoint, too. Give me your price. Give me your best price all when done edited. They may come up with $200, or $500, or whatever it is.

Now, you go ahead and you do the workshop, you kick butt. Now you've got a six, seven, eight-hour training system. Now you've got a system to sell. Now you can sell video and it could either be, you can do this online or offline. If it's going to be online, you've got the online video. You tell the video person, "Hey I want you to also take out the audio and I want people to be able to listen, too, if they want to listen in the car." You've got audio, you've got video, you can get it transcribed. You've got all the handouts and PowerPoints as a PDF file and you can do even worksheets and all that kind of stuff and sample routines. Now you've got an online system.

Or it can be physical. You can do DVD, CDs, workbooks, three-ring binder, and now you've got a system that you could sell for $300, $400, $500, $1,000, right, depending on if you're talking about ROI [return on investment] or not enough they're going to be able to make money with it and there you go. So now, two weeks from now, I'm ready, I'm locked and loaded and I've got a product. Then you go out and sell it. That's it. We talk about easy product creation, again it takes a little bit more work but the other alternative is for people to sit down, now I am going to do this and it never gets done. Oh, I have to record this. Oh, I can't do it. I have to watch the baby today and I'm on diaper duty and all this kind of crap happening.

ACTION ITEM REVIEW

Action Item

Create your life plan:

1. Grab a piece of paper.

Your Life Plan

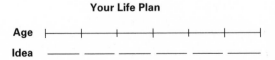

2. Draw a line in the middle.
3. Write your age at the far left.
4. Write five-year increments.
5. Place one idea in each section.

Look long term and realize that you have time to be patient.

Action Item

Get Your Right Idea in Four Steps

1. List 10 things you already know very well: Current job skills, hobbies, and so on.
2. List 10 ideas where you see a need.
3. List 10 industries you might want to work in: Passionate about, want to learn, and so on.
4. Take these lists and ideas, and grab a journal. Start to think about these industries and areas and see if there are any opportunities to solve a problem. Start talking to others in the industry and see if you can come up with your business idea. Write down a list of at least 10 problems that you can solve.

This step may take some time. That's okay, but give yourself a deadline on when you will need it complete by! Try it for about a week. Otherwise you will never actually pick an idea!

Finding problems to solve becomes easier as you tune into it more. Ideas can come out of the blue! So make sure you have that journal with you everywhere. (Or use your smartphone to keep track of the ideas.) I find the best ideas often come at night, just as I'm trying to go to sleep, or in the morning when I wake up. I also love thinking over ideas in the shower, or when I'm running. I've found the best places are when your body is busy but your mind can be quiet.

This is a process, and if you don't feel like you like any of the ideas you have come up with, start asking other people where they see a problem to be solved. I'm sure that will start to spark many ideas!

Action Item

Write out your ideal day. Be as detailed as possible. Keep it somewhere safe, like in a special journal so you can look back at it.

(I find looking back at it to be *amazing*!)

Action Item: Your Idea List Lifestyle Evaluation

Now it's time to grab that idea list. We want to check through each idea and figure out how it matches up to what your ideal lifestyle is like. There can be a big difference between offline businesses, or owning a physical location, and an online virtual business. These three steps help you figure out what side of things you like best.

1. Write down the ideas on the left.
2. Write down a quick synopsis of what your lifestyle might look like.
3. On a scale of 1 to 10 rate how close this lifestyle comes to your perfect lifestyle.

Idea	Lifestyle Like	Rating
1.		
2.		
3.		
4.		
5.		
6.		
7.		
8.		
9.		
10.		

The rating scale makes it easy to cross off ones that don't fit.

Action Item

1. Cross out any idea that is a rating of less than 7.
2. Fill out the worksheet. You can download the starter kit at http://EventualMillionaire.com/starterkit
3. Then go through the list of ideas you have and cross out the ones that don't fit with your lifestyle.

Action Item

Go through and eliminate the business ideas you have that do not fit with your ability to fund the start-up costs. If you have an amazing idea but the upfront costs are high, that doesn't mean don't do it if you think it's going to be huge. That just means you might need to get creative on funding it. We are so lucky to have websites that are crowd-funding platforms, like kickstarter.com or indiegogo.com. Websites like these can not only provide you with the start-up costs, but can also validate your idea! It's one of the best ways to start a new business that needs funding.

Action Item

Create a SWOT analysis for the top three business ideas you have. Delve into the competition that exists so you can see a clear picture of what you are up against.

Action Item

Just start the idea that looks the best right now.

Mentors, Masterminds, and Networking

I'm looking for mentors every day. People think there is your one mentor that helps you. I have many. I sought mentorship from everyone—from all-time winning coaches, to businessmen, to spiritual mentors.

—Ryan Blair, cofounder of ViSalus

Every successful person I have spoken to has had help of some kind. We cannot create amazing businesses or lifestyles all on our own. Nor should we!

You have probably heard this before, but surrounding yourself with successful people is critical. When I first started online I didn't have a great network and one of my goals was, "Gain a high-quality network of friends." I remember writing that in my journal and thinking, "Wow, I really don't have many people who are successful business owners that I could call *friends*." Acquaintances, yes. But not friends.

This was amazing to look back on. In just a few short years, my network has exploded. In fact, having a network of amazingly successful people is one thing I am known for. It is something that I specifically put a lot of effort into. I think it's been one of my keys to success toward designing my career and keeping me on my path as an Eventual Millionaire.

You have probably heard the phrase, "People do business with people they know, like, and trust." That is very true. But you know what is even better? People do business with friends! I think the landscape is changing. We are able to do business with people who are true friends.

Whenever I go out to find a mentor or a mastermind member I always look for someone who could be a friend first.

Millionaires Have Help!

Aaron Pitman's story on finding mentors:

JT: What do you tell someone who is working a job but feeling like, well, I've never been an entrepreneur before and there's so much to learn and this seems so difficult? What sort of advice do you have for them?

AP (Aaron Pitman): Find a mentor. I had a mentor, Robbie (granted I was 18, Robbie was 22, and he was broke at the time, but he still knew more than me). Sometimes it's just an outside perspective you need because a lot of times we overcriticize ourselves and give ourselves a hard time or we make ourselves innately a little bit more lazy. So we have a mentor to help push us forward. You'll have a much better success. I don't know of many rich people who don't have mentors.

JT: I agree with you 1,000 percent. Just from the interviews, it's a little ridiculous. So is Robbie your only mentor or have you found mentors before and after that?

AP: I have many, many mentors. I was so crazy as a kid building my entrepreneurial life that when I was out and about and if I ever saw a Ferrari or a Lamborghini or an Aston Martin or something like that, I would wait for that guy to come back or that girl to come back to their car. When they came in I would intercept them and say, "Hey my name is Aaron. I am an entrepreneur aspiring. I'm not successful yet but I want to be. Clearly by this car you're successful. Can I buy you a cup of coffee so I can ask you questions and learn from you?"

JT: Did they say yes?

AP: Yes, a lot of people said yes. Some people said no but the law of the averages, yes. A couple of those people actually ended up being investors of mine for certain projects and we invest together now. Yes.

Todd Tresidder, a millionaire founder of FinancialMentor .com [who is in my mastermind group, too!], said this about mastermind groups:

> A mastermind is an example of going pro where what you do is you build a structure that literally pulls your business forward. It keeps you from getting sidelined. It keeps you from getting distracted, because you're building a support system. You have a comfort zone of success that you're accustomed to and as you break through those thresholds, you need mechanisms to pull you through it. So that's the help of a mastermind group.

Mentors versus Coaches versus Mastermind Groups

There is a big difference between a mentor and mastermind group, though both are beneficial for different reasons. There is also a distinct difference between a mentor and a coach. Personally I have had many mentors, different coaches at different times and one mastermind group through it all.

A **mastermind group** is about four to seven of your peers, people in the trenches just like you, working on their businesses, learning, and growing. They're sharing current resources, tactics, and things that work for them, plus they give you support. Usually you meet on a schedule, either weekly or biweekly.

Napoleon Hill wrote the book *Think and Grow Rich*, which outlines the success principles of more than 500 millionaires who he interviewed. The book, which had sold more than 20 million copies at the time of his death, stresses the importance of mastermind groups too. (***Think and Grow Rich*** is the most recommended book by the millionaires I interviewed.)

A **mentor** is a trusted adviser or guide. You don't necessarily need to speak with him or her every week. A business mentor may help with high-level strategy in business, raising your level of confidence, pushing you out of your comfort zone, and more. Usually, a mentor is successful and has what you are trying to achieve. The best step in finding a mentor to take is to look to someone who already has what you want, and ask how he or she got it. Your mentor can teach you what worked and what didn't work. It will speed up your progress. Many people who are willing to mentor are doing it to give back and are not looking to charge you.

A **coach** is someone who is in the trenches with you. He or she works with you on a consistent basis to help bring you a desired result. Your coach is willing to hear the nitty-gritty about what you have on your plate and your to-do list, and can help create marketing plans, systems, and more for your business. A coach can also help with your level of personal development. Many times, issues that business owners have are related more to their thoughts and beliefs than the correct strategies to implement.

Mastermind Groups

Here is one example of how a mastermind group helped millionaire Tim Hamilton, owner of Astonished Designs. He was very open in his interview and explained the huge amount of fear he experienced as a business owner. One of the catalysts that helped him get past his fear was his mastermind group.

He said:

> My mastermind group was me and three other people who all wanted to grow. We all experienced some level of pain but we were separated by these forces in society that give us the information that we all have to appear totally competent, totally on top of things, totally together as if fear doesn't factor into our lives.
>
> There was one meeting when the four of us, in that room, decided to show each other that we were all vulnerable, struggling, and scared.
>
> That was what made all the difference in the world. We realized that if any one of us ever realized our greatest fear (which is essentially to lose everything), everyone's couch was open to everyone else who needed to sleep on it for a night.
>
> So I knew that at the end of the day that while my greatest fear of going out and living, ending out on the streets and just losing everything, it just was never going to happen.
>
> The most important part of that experience is that I realized that security actually comes from relationships.
>
> I thought it came from a certain amount of money, a signed contract, a verbal commitment from the next huge customer, but I think the greatest source of security comes from relationships.

How do you get involved in a mastermind group?

Well, there are many programs that you pay for that will give you a mastermind group. Some of them will be amazing and some of them will not be the right fit.

For me personally, I think you should start your own group. Then you have a say in the formation of the group, who is in it, and when it meets. Think long term. If this group is amazing, you will be with them for years.

You may be thinking, "What if I don't have an amazing group of successful friends to ask?" That's okay.

When I decided to go online I didn't know a lot about blogging or online marketing. I read a lot, and tried to take it all in. But I wanted to talk to people who knew what they were doing, who could help direct me. It's hard to know what is worth it and not worth it online.

I couldn't just go to a pool of friends I had because I only had one friend with online business success at the time. If you already have successful friends in business, think about creating a mastermind group with them.

I ended up with a stellar mastermind group of amazing people (and all but one were people I didn't know before I e-mailed them this!) by making a plan and taking action. In the next section I show you how, and that it's something you can adopt and use for yourself on your journey.

How to Create a Mastermind Group

You don't have to have a group of successful friends already. A mastermind group is an amazing way to increase the quality of your relationships with people who you want to be around more. When I started my mastermind group, I realized I didn't have a ton of friends who were where I wanted to be in business. So I made it a point to find some. Now my mastermind group includes diverse, amazing, successful people, including millionaires, and even a sword-swallowing hypnotist.

Here are the steps to set up your own mastermind group:

1. Find potential members.

You can find potential members almost anywhere. Locally or online, there are many amazing entrepreneurs who are looking to connect.

Make sure to invite people to the group who you think are much more successful than you. This can be tough if you feel like you don't have anything to offer them in return.

Just be sure that you include multiple members who are on equal levels. You want to make sure there isn't just one very successful person carrying the other members of your group. In that case, that one person will probably start to feel drained and leave. The best way is to find three to four other more successful people. That way, most of the group is on a similar playing field, and although you might be the one to get the most out of the group, it's your group, so you can set it up however you like! Also, once you have one very successful person committed, it's much easier to get other successful people to want to be a part.

If you are wondering why anyone might say yes to you at first, you probably don't give yourself enough credit. Think of some of the amazing things you have done before, and list them to entice new people to join.

The only online experience I had was when I worked with friends of mine who had a viral video online. In the e-mail to the potential members, I let them know that I had worked with these friends to up my credibility and I let them know where my strengths were.

Make sure the group will be highly valuable (like 10×!) to them. They do not need to spend their time doing things that won't return the value multiplied.

List 10 people in your extended network or peers who you don't know yet, but would be great for your mastermind group. Then choose one on the list and craft a simple short e-mail to that person.

Action Item

Download the template worksheet from http://EventualMillionaire.com/StarterKit.

1. List 10 people in your extended network or peers who you do not know yet but would be great for your mastermind group.
2. Now choose one person on the list and craft a simple, short e-mail to that person.

Here is a template:

Hello _____,

Qualifying sentence. (*Example:* I love your site, or I found you via my friend Joe on LinkedIn.)

Tell them about the group you are putting together and tell them you think they would be a great addition. (*Example:* I'm putting together a new mastermind group of like-minded business owners to help each other grow our businesses. I think you would be a great fit for the group.)

You can also include a bit more about a mastermind group, mention you have a document with the guidelines if they wanted more information, or actually include the document attached.

Your quick bio listing achievements and successes, or other members of the groups bios listing their achievements. (*Example:* I own a publishing business and I've been able to get clients on the Amazon best-seller list.)

Once you start to have amazing people say yes, use their great achievements to get even bigger businesses in the group.

Write an end greeting explaining how great it would be to keep in touch. (*Example:* I understand if you can't fit it into your packed schedule, but I just wanted to offer it to you since you have a great business.)

Your name
Your URL
Your social media links (if you have them!)

3. Send out crafted e-mails to at least five of the people on your list this week.

Make sure to follow up promptly with each response. Also make a note in your calendar to e-mail at least three or four mentors or possible mastermind participants each week until you have the support you need.

It's only an e-mail. It's very simple. You never know what could come from it. Many of my *key* relationships came from this exact method.

2. Create a structure and format for the group.

Mastermind groups usually don't have a leader, but you will have to take that role in the beginning to get the group together. (Included here are the outlines for a basic mastermind format with a hot seat. It also includes ways to keep each other accountable with goals.)

Mastermind Guidelines

- Each meeting will be held on Monday at 12:00 P.M. Eastern (9 A.M. Pacific) for 60 minutes. (Choose a time that works for everyone.)
- It is expected that each member be present and on time for the meeting. If someone cannot attend please e-mail me ahead of time.
- Everyone will have an opportunity to speak within the framework of the group. It works best if each member participates equally.
- Everyone is here to support each other. Please keep in mind there will be constructive criticism, but there should be no putting down, or criticism of other group members. It should be an open and positive experience for all.
- It is important to note, the mastermind is not just for advice, but it also becomes a positive place where you can manifest your goals with a group. Every person should make it their intention to support the individual goals and help manifest them.

Mastermind Outline

12:00 Welcome/Agenda
12:05 Sharing a "win" from the previous week
12:20 Hot Seat—one member
- What are you working on?
- What's working for you?
- With what do you need help?
12:40 Last questions
- Who can help (member) with their problem?
12:50 Resource
12:55 State your goal for the next week
1:00 End

Action Item

Create a list of 20 possible members for the mastermind group.

Being Open and Honest

If you are in a group of more successful people, you may have a tendency to hold back or feel like you aren't good enough. Just remember that no matter where you are on your journey, you are valuable, and your worldview and ideas will benefit the group. Being open and honest in your group will allow you to get more out of it.

One step past being just open and honest is being vulnerable. When you become comfortable enough with your mastermind group to talk about your fears, the things that you don't really want to tell, that can create a trust and friendship that goes well beyond business. Plus, it allows the other group members to help you more, and once you are all sharing it lets you know that you are not alone in your fears!

Mentors

You might be asking, "Why would a mentor even want to work with me?"

You may be telling yourself, "I haven't done anything yet! I'm not big. I don't have money to pay them." But it's not about what you have already done, and I believe you shouldn't have to pay your mentors.

When I asked Amy Applebaum, a business coach and millionaire, she said:

> It is about enrolling people in your vision. If they're not enrolled in your vision, they will not participate. But most people love to help. There's help right in front of us.
> It can be a friend's family member. It can be a friend of a friend. It can be someone who is a business associate. You just want to aim high.
>
> You need a really successful person that's more behind the scenes so that they have access and will give you time.
>
> You must show your commitment or strength or it will never happen. That means being committed to listening to them when they do respond.
>
> Take action on what they say. No one wants their great advice to fall on deaf ears.

How to Get Your Own Mentor

> I lucked out; I had a good mentor when I was 19. Otherwise, I'd probably be working for somebody.
>
> —MATT KUBANCIK, STREET MODA
> ($6.8 MILLION IN REVENUE AT AGE 25)

Finding a mentor is somewhat similar to getting a mastermind group, except that you don't need to formally ask that person to be a mentor. Many times, you may start to build relationships with people in such a way that you could call them a mentor even though neither one of you officially asked!

Now, a mentor is someone you don't necessarily seek to be your best friend. Mentors are people you can ask for advice occasionally, and they will respond. You want someone who is at a very high level, who is where you want to be in a few years' time. Hopefully, the mentor will give you insider knowledge for strategy and planning.

Finding My Mentor

Getting a mentor is partly on you to take the initiative to ask for advice. The other part is an organic relationship that can grow from a chance encounter. Here is how I got two amazing mentors:

Before I had any real experience in my business, I decided I wanted to talk to the competition. The competition was a 60-year-old man, and I was a 27-year-old gal (who looked about 18). Asking for his advice put me on the fast track to where I am now.

I don't know where I would have been if I wasn't willing to send the e-mail to him.

One day, while I was looking up potential competitors who were local, I found Kurk Lalemand. He spoke at all of the local events, and was well known in the community. I was a bit intimidated reading about him. He had sold a million-dollar business, and had a great network already.

I decided to send him an e-mail on a whim. I mentioned that I had recently moved to the area and was getting into coaching and found him. I laid out a few questions for him in the email. Shortly after, I received an e-mail back from him asking to set up a time to chat. Our meeting that was supposed to be an hour lasted more than two hours.

He ended up giving me a ton of advice on who to target in the area and where I should be connected. I thought it was amazing that he was so willing to give advice. I left his office thinking how great our meeting went, so I decided to send him a thank you note. I just wanted to thank him for all of the time he gave me.

I was surprised when a few days later I received an e-mail from him, asking about a possible mentor/apprentice role. When we met about it, he said the thank you card I sent really sealed the deal about asking. Even though he was looking to mentor someone who was much older than I was, he was really impressed.

I ended up working for free for him for a few hours a week for six months; in exchange he taught me everything he knew. Because he was a coach and a mentor he was able to push me and help me grow personally. The growth I experienced in those months was exponential. He had me cold calling, doing cold walk-ins, public speaking, and really stepping out of my comfort zone.

I've found many mentors since. I would say at least 15 of the millionaires I interviewed mentioned that if there was any way they could help just to ask. I've chatted for many hours with them after the phone calls on specific business issues I have. I've been able to lean on them and their experience countless times.

How Millionaires Found Their Mentors

The stories on getting a mentor vary and a lot of it is luck and coincidence. But you will see some themes from these stories. Successful people want to help, and all you have to do is find a synergy with someone successful that you connect with.

Matt Kubanick from Street Moda's Story

> MK (Matt Kubanick): I always kind of had a passion for fashion so I started Street Moda by myself when I was 18, in high school, and when I was 19, I was in a warehouse. Had two employees and I met a mentor who has been my mentor ever since. His name is Jerry and he has been in the shoe business for 45 years. I met him when I was 19. Wasn't very successful from 18 to 19 and he kind of transformed my life—the old-school shoe mentality. He had businesses in New York and Chicago and really transformed my life so

I kind of took the Internet marketing aspect and fashion knowledge I had and just kind of developed it myself along with his guidance as a business advisor because I never went to college.

He taught me how to talk to manage people; everything you would learn in college out of a textbook he taught me real life. He had a lot of connections in the shoe business so that helped a lot with vendor relationships. He helped how to manage, how to hire people, how to treat people.

JT: So he came to you? You didn't go searching for him?

MK: No, it was just kind of ironic. His wife at the time made him retire. He located me through a big article in a local business journal that they wrote up on our business and said, "Look I've been in the shoe business 45 years" and said, "I'd like to help you out." It just kind of started from there.

JT: Imagine where you'd be right now if you didn't get that piece of press and he never saw it. Do you think you might be working for someone else?

MK: I would have probably, I made a lot of mistakes and he has at least saved me a few million dollars minimum. But I still don't tell him everything. It's still a constant battle like any relationship.

JT: You don't pay him, right?

MK: No, no. We worked out an agreement that's based really upon the performance once again—incentive-based agreement—based upon the performance of the company. So no, I didn't give up any ownership stake, but I worked out something that as a company grows and as the company he makes a percentage of that and he's still in here every other day—two/three days a week—for a few hours a day and advising.

It has kind of gotten to the point where he's working with my vice president and high-level employees a lot more and really working with them and working for our accountants and that sort of thing. We still talk a lot on business trips but we're not in here meeting two to three hours a day like we were. He has definitely been a huge asset to me.

Doug Guller, Owner of Bikinis Bar and Grill, on Finding Advice from Successful People in the Same Industry

DG (Doug Guller): That was a big reason why I believe that we've been fortunate to have the growth that we've had at the beginning. When I landed here, I didn't know anybody. I started asking people "Who are the best restaurateurs? Who are the best bar owners? Give me their names, their numbers, who knows them. Get me an intro."

It was using my sales skills from prior and networking that worked. I probably met with almost 10 business owners and I said, "Hey my name is Doug, I just moved here. I want to open a restaurant. I was wondering if you have five minutes so I could ask you a couple questions."

That initial five-minute meeting was an hour or more and I still talk to a lot of those folks. I realized that my questions were basic, looking back at it. I mean, probably laughable questions to those folks but they were really genuine and gave me a lot of time and a lot of good input and steered me in the right direction.

I would say some were giving advice but mostly they were sharing their experiences and that was good for me because from there I could deduce what I wanted to do.

JT: So your competition is willing to talk to you about their advice when you're going to be competing with them? Were they just completely open or did you get people who rejected you and said, "I'm not going to talk to you because you're going to be my competition down the street"?

DG: I think it was the name, and honestly it's part of the reason I chose the name. The name Bikinis is so thought-provoking and shocking to folks and it creates this image that immediately helped me to get a return phone call.

"I'm Doug. I'm opening a place called Bikinis." They just called me back because they wanted to hear the story. It just sounds funny and laughable so they were like I got to hear what this guy has to say.

What they realized during the conversation was that I wasn't going to directly compete with them. There weren't any like me at the time that were big in Austin. There were a few that existed, but I certainly didn't go to them to ask for advice. There were other sports bars, like a Buffalo Wild Wings, but again I didn't go there since it's such a big company.

I was looking for the small business owner. Someone I could really relate to and who I knew I'd be trying to get into their shoes. So I went to restaurants, but it was maybe an Italian restaurant or it was a bar that was strictly not even serving food because I knew that since it was that type of business it would be pretty close to what I was going to do, which was find a building, find managers, build a menu, sign a lease. All those types of things. It got me into the ballpark and then I could get specific with what I was looking to do.

How Derek Sivers, Millionaire and CD Baby Creator, Connects with Potential Mentors Here is part of the transcript from Derek's interview:

DS (Derek Sivers): I think it's when you get a real mutual admiration thing. When somebody who you really look up to, is really a role model to you, and they like you, too, and they give you an open channel. "Anytime you have a question feel free to ask" kind of thing. So I've had that with a few people, Seth Godin, for example.

There was a great moment where I was a huge fan of his books and at CD Baby we used to get 200 to 300 orders a day and we had to process them. It was kind of factory style. It would just get turned out.

We had 50 people working in the warehouse and every now and then I would just peek in on the day's orders by scanning the list of everything going out that day. There was one day back in 2003 or 2004, something like that, that I just happened to be scanning through the customer list and it said, "Seth Godin." I thought, "No way. Maybe there's another."

But it said his e-mail address and it was going to an address in New York. So I sent him an e-mail. I said, "Dear Mr. Godin, I'm a huge fan of yours." He wrote back saying, "Dear Mr. Sivers, I'm a huge fan of yours. I love CD Baby, I think it's brilliant. I think it's absolutely amazing what you've done," and then in his next two or three books he would often use me as an example.

We had a real kind of mutual admiration thing and still do to this day. Just a few weeks ago I told him something about what an honor it is that I'm able to talk to him anytime and he said, "You know, you got it all wrong, it's backwards. It's an honor for me to be able to talk to you anytime."

Every now and then you have amazing things like that that just happen by chance that aren't any kind of official mentorships but just friends.

JT: Do you have any advice for people who maybe haven't created a multimillion-dollar business to get the attention of Seth Godin or, in general, people who have smaller businesses that are really looking for mentors or at least just an open channel to talk to someone?

DS: Definitely: just ask. You'd be surprised how effective a simple three-sentence e-mail can be. I think a three- or four-sentence e-mail is so effective and respectful that if you send a real quick pointed three sentence e-mail, who could not answer it? Unless somebody really has their block gates up and they don't read their own e-mail, but I think anybody who reads their own e-mail . . . I've sent other e-mails off to my favorite authors and they have no idea who I am and I don't include my website, they've never heard of CD Baby or anything like that, and I've been amazed how well the three-sentence e-mail can get a reply.

Just a one-sentence qualification like "I'm a huge fan of your books and, this one changed the way I think." Question number two or sentence two, a simple direct question like "I have one question—Do you feel that a business should split into multiple parts once it gets over 50 employees or do you feel that that was just in your case only? Any reply appreciated. Thank you." Something like that.

I think if you send somebody a simple direct question, not trying to dump the weight of your life on them or anything but just asking a simple direct question, you get a reply. And sometimes you can go back and forth like that a few times and maybe then if you've just got a URL in your signature and they're trying to answer the question, "Well, who is this asking?" and they go to your URL and there's some interesting posts there or you've shared your philosophies or your company and what you're doing is interesting, it may lead to more or it may just be somebody who answers your questions when you ask.

I've had it both ways. I get a couple hundred e-mails a day and I reply to them all. Often I have no idea who I'm e-mailing. I'm not replying to them because they are somebody, I'm just replying to them because they e-mailed. So I do my best to give a helpful answer not based on any qualification of who they are but just because they asked. I've been really surprised how reachable people are when you just send a nice simple e-mail. On the other hand, if you send one of those five-page-long e-mails then don't be surprised if you don't get a reply because it's just too hard to reply.

Derek laid out for me what he says when he e-mails potential mentors and successful people.

Here are a few of the keys:

- Keep it very short. Successful people don't have time for long e-mails. (If it's long, it will be ignored!)
- Don't ask them something that a simple Google search will answer. (You cannot waste their time!)
- Show them that you like their work, in a deeper way than just saying, "I love your work/book/company!"

Use the template below to find your mentors.

Action Item

Create a list of 10 possible mentors. Find their e-mail addresses and e-mail them.

1. List 10 people in your extended network already that would make a good mentor. (Think of acquaintances, old friends, friends of friends, people on LinkedIn or Facebook.)

2. List 10 people you admire who have done exactly what you want to do and might seem out of reach (smaller book authors, business owners, etc.). Search LinkedIn, Facebook, and your industry's magazines.

3. Choose one person on the list and craft a simple, short e-mail to that person.

Hello _____,

Qualifying sentence (*Example:* I'm a huge fan of your books or you know my friend Joe and he said you might have experience in this that could help me.)

    A simple direct question in a sentence or two that you could not find out online easily. (*Example:* But I have one question—Do you feel that a business should split into multiple parts once it gets more than 50 employees or do you feel that that was just in your case only?)

    Write an end greeting reinstating how thankful you are. (*Example:* Any reply appreciated, or thank you in advance.)

Your name
Your URL
Your social media links (if you have them!)

4. Send out crafted e-mails to at least five of the people on your list this week.

Interview Them

Andrew Warner of Mixergy.com thinks the best way to learn from others is to interview them. I highly agree!

    He said:

What I suggest is find someone who you admire. It doesn't have to be the most admired person in your life, but someone you admire, and then go and ask them for a few minutes to ask them questions.

    Now here's the thing, if you do that, they're going to say no because you're probably a nobody and they're obviously someone who is worthy of the admiration or else you wouldn't be asking them. The reason they are going to say no is there's not anything in it for them and there's a whole lot in it for you and it's going to suck up their time. So the way you get them to say yes is you offer to publish it somewhere so that they get something. So that if they are going to give you words of wisdom, if they're going to give you encouragement, they're not just going to be speaking to you. They're going to be speaking to the thousands of people—maybe even tens of thousands, depending on who you find—who don't have the guts to ask them the way that you just did.

I would say find the person you admire, ask them to do an interview—be selfish with the questions, because other people are going to have similar questions—and then publish it. If you don't have your own blog—I went to Mashable when I didn't have an audience and I said, "Can I publish it on your site?" Find someone out there who is going to let you publish this interview with someone you admire and you're going to find yourself both learning directly and making a connection that could end up being a lifelong friendship or a lifelong mentorship and through the audience that then connects with what you've done with that interview, you're going to find yourself reaching people who you never could connect with otherwise, who will help you sometimes in ways that you can't predict. That's the goal. Go out there and do what I do every day, do what Jaime does every day. Don't just watch us, do it.

Andrew and I, and anyone with an interview show, are able to connect with people who normally we would never have access to. This is a great way to ask whatever questions you want to people with the experience you need!

I love to ask specific questions about my business or my husband's business while on the interview.

It's also a great marketing tactic for your business. You can check out one of my businesses (donecast.com or 21daypodcast .com) to learn how to start your own interview show.

Does Not Having a Mentor = Failure?

No, not at all!
Many of the millionaires didn't have any mentors.
When I asked MJ Demarco if he had a mentor, he said:

No, my mentors were the books I was reading weekly. Guys like
Tony Robbins, Les Brown, and Jim Rohn.

More than one third (39 percent) of the millionaires I surveyed
didn't have mentors, so don't think you cannot succeed without
one!

I will say things can be a lot easier if you do. But don't get
caught up on needing one first before you dig into your business.

Networking

You don't need to connect with people just to be in a mastermind
group or to find a mentor. Increasing your network with amazing
people is like building a powerful asset. You may not even need to
use the asset now, but it will exist for you for many years if you take
care of it. Even with future businesses.

> You always hear "oh this guy just came out of nowhere and is
> an overnight success." Well it's not really like that because, you
> can ask my buddy Billy Murphy, a lot of people thought he was
> an overnight success with Blue Fire Poker. That's not true. He
> spent years developing his skills at poker and networking and
> that industry and meeting other professional poker players to
> build his network.
>
> He couldn't have just started Blue Fire Poker like that,
> if he didn't know how to play poker professionally and make
> money at it and he didn't have the contacts.
> —BOBBY CASEY, CEO OF GLOBAL WEALTH PROTECTION
> (ABOUT BILLY MURPHY)

I surveyed the millionaires and found that only 15 percent of
them had existing networks that they could tap into when they started
their businesses. Most of their responses sounded like Scott Skinger's,
"No. When I started TrainSignal I was completely on my own and
didn't have any connections in the education or business world."

So don't worry about starting from scratch, but do realize that
putting an effort in to build your network of possible prospects,
partnerships, and just friendships will help your business grow.

Online Connections

We are so connected now, it's insane. That's how I can live in a town of 2,000 people and have more Facebook fans than there are people living in my town. We don't need to live in New York City or Los Angeles to be well connected. In fact, when I go to conference people assume I'm from NYC or LA when they start talking to me, especially when we have so many similar friends from those places.

We are so fortunate!

That also means we are dealing with overcommunication. We get requests from many different platforms like Twitter, LinkedIn, or Facebook and so many people want to be our friends, or fans, or connections. Even today face-to-face interaction is the best way to form true friendships. But we can carry out these friendships online.

Even locally! You can meet at a local business event and follow up online. Here is what Chris Gravagna, serial entrepreneur and CEO of Wine by Wives, said about networking:

> CG (Chris Gravagna): My Twitter is @iamchrisemedia. I think I just hit 2,600 follows yesterday.
>
> Having 2,600 followers is a pretty decent feat done all organically and without these things that get you followers. I really went out and drove these followers through good content, good information and driving the value. LinkedIn is a very important part of my life. I drive a lot of relationships there. I do a lot of networking. When I look at social media, social media is like hypergrowth networking because I do a lot of networking.
>
> I'm out there, constantly driving, doing events, meeting real people, shaking hands but then I'll go back and take that business card then I'll see if they have a LinkedIn account. I'll see if they are on Facebook and I'll see if they are on Twitter. Then I'll continue to interact on a digital level and then personal level with those people so that there are constant touch points. I've seen that be very successful for me.

JT: Excellent. That's great advice. I think we sort of try and use
       social media as a replacement for regular in-person network-
       ing but the fact that you are using in-person networking and
       just social media as the touch point and connection seems to
       work a lot better, right?

CG: It works a lot better. Nothing is going to replace interper-
       sonal interaction with people. I mean nothing is going to
       replace that. Those relationships that you are able to nur-
       ture and you are able to facilitate are so important to driving
       success and driving relationships. But having that constant
       hyperconnectivity through the social media platform helps
       you in nurturing that relationship. It helps you in creating a
       high level of that relationship and driving that instant com-
       munication with those people.

Action Item

Take one action to increase the size of your network. That
may mean adding a networking event to your calendar
right now, or planning to go to a conference.

Or that might mean you need to get back in touch with some people
who you have been meaning to for a long time but it wasn't your top
priority. Until now. Pick that one action, and do it.

Asking for Help

Sometimes just asking for help is one of the hardest things for an
entrepreneur to do. We are a stubborn bunch who think we can
do it all ourselves without any help. We can figure it out. We don't
need to rely on anyone else.

And you don't.

But if you want a more enjoyable *life*, which as an Eventual
Millionaire you do, then make it easy on yourself. Be okay with asking for help, and connecting with people. Get support. Do at least
one of the action items in this chapter *right now*.

ACTION ITEM REVIEW

Action Item

1. List 10 people in your extended network or peers that you do not know yet but would be great for your mastermind group.
2. Now choose one person on the list and craft a simple, short e-mail to that person.

Here is a template:

Hello _____,

Qualifying sentence. (*Example:* I love your site, or I found you via my friend Joe on LinkedIn.)
    Tell them about the group you are putting together and tell them you think they would be a great addition. (*Example:* I'm putting together a new mastermind group of like-minded business owners to help each other grow our businesses. I think you would be a great fit for the group.)
    You can also include a bit more about a mastermind group, mention you have a document with the guidelines if they wanted more information, or actually include the document attached.
    Your quick bio listing achievements and successes, or other members of the groups bios listing their achievements. (*Example:* I own a publishing business and I've been able to get clients on the Amazon best seller list.)
    Once you start to have amazing people say yes, use their great achievements to get even bigger businesses in the group.
    Write an end greeting explaining how great it would be to keep in touch. (*Example:* I understand if you can't fit it into your packed schedule but I just wanted to offer it to you since you have a great business.)

Your name
Your URL

Your social media links (if you have them!)

3. Send out crafted e-mails to at least five of the people on your list this week.

    Make sure to follow up promptly with each response. Also make a note in your calendar to e-mail at least three or four mentors or possible mastermind participants each week until you have the support you need.

    It's only an e-mail. It's very simple. You never know what could come from it. Many of my *key* relationships came from this exact method.

Action Item

Create a list of 20 possible members for the mastermind group.

Action Item

Create a list of 10 possible mentors. Find their e-mail addresses and e-mail them!

1. List 10 people in your extended network already that would make a good mentor. (Think of acquaintances, old friends, friends of friends, people on LinkedIn or Facebook.)
2. List 10 people you admire that have done exactly what you want to do and might seem out of reach (smaller book authors, business owners, etc.). Search LinkedIn, Facebook, and your industries magazines.
3. Choose one person on the list and craft a simple, short e-mail to that person.

Hello _____,

Qualifying sentence. (*Example:* I'm a huge fan of your books or you know my friend Joe and he said you might have experience in this that could help me.)

A simple direct question in a sentence or two that you could not find out online easily. (*Example:* But I have one question— Do you feel that a business should split into multiple parts once it gets more than 50 employees or do you feel that that was just in your case only?)

Write an end greeting reinstating how thankful you are. (*Example:* Any reply appreciated, thank you in advance.)

Your name
Your URL
Your social media links (if you have them!)

4. Send out crafted e-mails to at least five of the people on your list this week.

Action Item

Take one action to increase the size of your network. That may mean adding a networking event to your calendar right now, or planning to go to a conference.

Or that might mean you need to get back in touch with some people who you have been meaning to for a long time but it wasn't your top priority. Until now. Pick that one action, and do it.

CHAPTER

Long Business Plans Are for Banks

So many times people sit down and they start writing a business plan like they're writing a novel. It's just the worst thing you can possibly do.
—Michael Burcham

Do you need a business plan? In this chapter you will learn a quick way to plan your business, based on how millionaires plan theirs. It can be a bit overwhelming at times to start a business, and to know what you need to do first, and what you can save for later. Don't worry, you won't be creating an inch thick report of what you want your business to be!

When I surveyed the millionaires on whether they started with a business plan, they had some common (and sometimes funny!) answers.

> Ha Ha, LOL. No freaking way.
> Nothing formal, more in my head than anything else.
> Nope.
> No. I actually have never had one.
> No. I didn't know what the hell I was doing at the time. Now I will put outlines together when starting a new business.
> No. I learned that a business plan was a good idea when I joined Entrepreneurs Organization in the early 2000s, but never took them seriously before that.

No. I never start with a business plan but I believe they are incredibly important. Since I have had plenty of business experience I usually know what to do next but I want to repeat some sort of a business plan is smart. My business plans have always started with a pad of paper and strategies that I want to implement as I move forward.

No, just a drive.

No. I had some back-of-napkin calculations, but I pretty much just jumped right in with some very naive assumptions about how business worked.

In our heads, yes. On paper, no.

No. Just always knew I was in a service business and serviced the crap out of people.

No. I was just operating from trial and error to figure out what worked.

No. To start a business you need only one thing—a customer. If you are providing enough value that someone is willing to pay you for it, you have a business. The rest you just figure out as you go. I've only ever developed business plans for ventures that required funding from banks or investors. It is a sales document meant to convince the investors and bankers you have planned out what you are going to do with "their" money.

Not really, big believer planning is guessing and not worth most of the time you put into it.

Most of the ones who did say yes didn't do a traditional business plan:

Not a traditional business plan. It is my own version. I always have a strategic plan with action steps, but I don't waste time formulating documents just to gather dust on a shelf. My plans are working documents that govern day to day activities.

Yes, I always have a plan of attack but as any business goes things change as you get more involved and realize what is working and what is not.

Yes. Although I did not have a formal business plan laid out, I set goals and stuck with it until I achieved them.

Yes. We wrote it on a paper table cloth in an Italian restaurant. It contained our name, our mission, vision, services, target customers, and values. Very simple.

Do you see a theme?

Most millionaires did *not* have a 30-page business plan like the Small Business Association (SBA) suggests. In fact, many had no plan at all, and others had some scribbled notes on a napkin. A few had in-depth business plans, but that didn't necessarily help them. Dustin Wells, founder of Headspring, had an award-winning business plan, but it failed miserably. President and CEO of Sandstorm Gold and Sandstorm Metals Nolan Watson needed an in-depth business plan—but only to show to banks he was looking to get loans from.

That doesn't mean that having a 30-page business plan is bad. It's a good idea to do research and be knowledgeable, but you don't need to document 30 pages of research and planning before you start to take action and figure out if your business idea has legs.

I personally think the 30-page business plan is a procrastination tool. When I first started, I thought that's what all businesses did. I read the SBA, I downloaded its really big template. I spent weeks filling it out, but in all that time I never actually went out and talked to my market.

Derek Sivers said:

> You can have plans, but once your plans hit the real world, the real world tells you what it wants, and it's often not what you had planned. That means that you can spend forever writing a plan for the next year, but as soon as you get it out there, things happen, and your plan will likely change. You cannot predict or plan on things one year or five years out with that much degree of certainty. You can set goals and have ideas, but in the end, the real world tells you what it wants.

Most millionaires started their businesses with what I call a *Square Business Plan*. When I distilled what was on their two- to three-page business plans, these were the components. It's also not something set in stone; it's something that is continually updated. As you get more information from your markets about what they want, and what you might be able to charge, and so on, you learn more and can update the plan with better information.

Here are a few examples of millionaires who did not use 30-page business plans:

Brenton Hayden, Founder of Renters Warehouse: The Inc. 500 List of Fastest-Growing Companies

Brenton has started more than 18 businesses. He has attended Harvard Business School and MIT. He said, "I don't like making business plans more than about two or three pages. It's never this awesome, well-put-together presentation. It's a lot of printouts from the Internet. It's a lot of scribbled notes, napkins, Post-It notes, whatever. It's what you know in advance before you start a business."

Doug Guller, Founder of Bikinis Bar and Grill: From Zero to 600 Employees, and Owning More than 13 Restaurants in Five Years

Doug didn't have a Harvard Degree, but he did have a background in finance. He said, "I didn't write a full-blown business plan. It was more of probably a two- to three-page document that had bullet points about the specific areas of the restaurant or what I learned from people."

Both of these millionaires are saying that you need to know a lot about the business *before* you write your business plan. That's why the Square Business Plan comes *after* we gained feedback from our target customers.

The Square Business Plan

Now you are ready for a step-by-step action plan on how to plan your business. There are a few things to do before the plan begins, like naming your business and creating your business structure, but then it's time to dig into creating the business itself.

Legend for the Square Business Plan

Avatar: Your end buyer of your product or service.

USP: Unique selling point—your main selling point that is unique.

Key differentiator: The main thing that separates you from your competition.

KPI: Key performance indicator—A number that you track (could be sales, or profit, or clients, etc.) to see the health of your business at a glance.

Business metric: A measurement that helps you keep track of your goals.

Launch strategy: How you plan to bring your product to market.

Marketing: Where you reach your prospects and try to persuade them to purchase your product or service.

Sales: Where you are actually asking for your prospect to buy your product.

Action Item: Square Business Plan

Table 6.1   Square Business Plans

Mission Statement	USP/Key Differentiator
Avatar	Resources Available

Business Metric	Launch Strategy
Metric #1	#1
Metric #2	#2
Metric #3	#3

Download the Square Business Plan at http://EventualMillionaire.com.

Table 6.1 is an outline of the Square Business Plan. You will be filling in these sections and there is a link to download this template below.

These are the key pieces you need when you start a business.

Mission Statement

A mission statement is more than just what service or product your business provides, so it can get overwhelming to try to come up with that perfect message, especially if you are trying to keep it to only one or two sentences.

To wrap their heads around crafting their mission statements, millionaires like to figure out their *why*. Why is this company in business? Who is it here to serve? How is it helping people?

Michael Stelzner of SocialMediaExaminer.com started a new business. His newest mission statement was: "Project Torch helps solve the question posed by _____. We do so by empowering this audience to effortlessly create impactful _____." (The project was so new that he wasn't able to talk details with us, so he gave us this template!)

ACTION ITEM

Action Item

Brainstorm your why. Then write down many ideas for how it helps people.

Start to play with possible mission statements. Write down 5 to 10 and see which ones resonate most strongly with your gut feeling.

_____

_____

_____

_____

_____

_____

_____

_____

_____

_____

Key Differentiator

What makes you different from your competitors?

Why should I pick you over everybody else, especially if they are doing similar things or the same things?

Brenton Hayden of Renters Warehouse said:

> When I start a business, I like innovation. I want a key differen-
> tiator. What's going to make us different? What's really going to
> be our value proposition? Why would somebody choose us over
> somebody else? What comes back to my plan is what is your
> key differentiator? What's your value proposition? How big of
> a market is it? Who is going to be your customer? I always start
> with the who, what, where, when, and why and how.

Matthew Tuttle, founder, chief executive officer, and chief
investment officer of Tuttle Wealth Management, LLC, said:

> Number one is you've got to differentiate yourself. I don't mean
> just slight hey I'm up here I'm a little bit different. I mean serious
> substantial differentiation where someone who's not in your busi-
> ness would say, okay I see what that guy does is totally different
> than what the other people do because what I found and really in
> any industry that's worth being in that there will be competition.

You Are the Differentiator   In some circumstances *you* are the key differentiator. If you are looking to be an author, speaker, or expert in your
field, being you is enough. You just have to let the *you* shine through.

Michael Port, author of the best-selling books *Book Yourself Solid*
and *Think Big Manifesto,* said:

> You hear people talk about the unique selling proposition. You
> got to have a unique selling proposition and that particular
> term works very, very well when you're developing some sort
> of physical product or restaurant or something that the con-
> sumer is buying without strong connection to the creator of
> the product. But when people are buying something because
> of the connection to the creator of the product like a book or a
> speech or coaching or mentoring consulting, whatever it is, the
> way that the person sells that, the way that that coach or author
> or whomever, the way that they sell that is by being more them-
> selves because that's what makes them distinct.
>
> That's the unique selling proposition. It's not trying to be
> different. It's not trying to be distinct. It's be more yourself. If
> you can be more yourself, there's nobody else who is going to
> be like you so that's unique. Through that process, you'll see
> why you're unique selling proposition is very strong.

That doesn't mean you can have an inferior product, or service, but it does mean that people connect with other *people*. Michael Port is a shining example of this. Michael is down to earth, and transparent in all of his books and speeches. You come to *like* him. And that's a way that he separates himself from other speakers. Michael is someone you would want to be friends with.

Amy Applebaum is a coach and speaker with her own brand at AmyApplebaum.com; she does a great job letting her personality come through. She strives to make everyone feel welcome, and she is extremely genuine. She almost seems like a big sister ready to help. These things come through in her brand, too.

Michael Hyatt of MichaelHyatt.com also does this. Not only does he create amazing content, but he lets his experience and personality show through as an expert. He cares deeply about you, and about helping you get the most out of your life. His podcast is even called "This Is Your Life"! His brand and his personality are one.

Avatar

Who specifically are you creating your product or service for?

You need to understand your potential customers, not only to understand what they want in your product or service, but also to understand the best way to find them and how to talk to them. You will also save more money because your marketing will be more of a sniper rifle than a buckshot!

I interviewed Carissa Reiniger, who owns a company called Silver Lining. She has walked thousands of business owners through her Silver Lining Action Plan (SLAP). One of the core pieces of a SLAP is finding out who your avatar is.

Avatar: The embodiment of an idea.

So you think about that huge market that you want to target, and you choose one person that acts as the face. That way you are writing to only one person. You are looking for that one person in all of your marketing and sales tactics.

Carissa said:

> So many business owners spend so much energy walking and talking to the wrong person because they haven't identified who their ideal client is. So your "who" is your ideal client and at Silver Lining we go to the point where we actually build an avatar for that person, we give them a name—so there's 10,000 business owners out there walking around with an imaginary friend.

I always think that people think I'm married to this guy named James or I'm dating someone named James. James is Silver Lining's ideal client, so in our scenario James is in his early forties, he's been in business for at least a couple of years, he's got over $100,000 but less than $2 million in revenue, he's self-made, he's an owner/operator business, he's got under 10 employees and he really wants to grow and he's frustrated by this cash flow capacity catch-22 that he's in and he wants to figure out how to get out of it and move beyond it. That's our ideal client. Do 100 percent of our clients look exactly like that? No. But am I going to spend a minute of my time or a dollar of my money if James is not going to be on the other end? When I'm asked to speak at an event I ask if James will be there, and if James isn't going to be there, I don't go.

Finding Your Avatar

What are the benefits of your product or service? _____
Who would benefit most from it? _____
What are some of their characteristics?
> Age _____
> Gender _____
> Occupation _____
> Location _____
> Education _____
> Family Status _____
What are their psychographics?
> Values _____
> Behavior _____
> Lifestyle _____
> Attitude _____
> Hobbies _____

Finding your target market is a process, too! Not everyone does their research before they jump into a business. Even millionaires! Do your best at this point.

Metrics

Working out your metrics for your business plan doesn't necessarily mean projections for the first years. You would just be guessing at this point if you tried. It does mean, however, figuring out what key financial numbers you will be looking at to determine the health of your company.

KPIs are key performance indicators. They are numbers that you look at to understand if things are going well in your business, or not so well. These can include quantities like gross profit, or net profit, number of new prospects, number of products sold, break-even point, plus many more. At this point, you should be establishing which numbers you'll use as your KPIs. It's about finding out what key measurements your specific company will need to look at and set goals with.

Michael Burcham, serial entrepreneur who runs the Nashville Entrepreneur Center, said:

> Think of financial **metrics** as a scorecard of the game called *entrepreneurship*. You can watch football but if there were no scoreboard and no one ever kept score, you just watch as you run up and down the field all the time. That's why the second accountant's score counts. All the financial metrics of a business are a scorecard and it lets you know are you winning or losing at this game.
>
> So even before you begin the game, setting a basis of what you expect to do and then beating that is an incredible way to keep score on yourself to make sure the time and money you're spending to refine this idea is going to matter in the next six months, year, year and a half.

Action Item

Choose three key performance indicators to start measuring in this new company. If you have an online e-commerce company, it might be visitors, conversion rates, and revenue.

Revenue Model

To be a "business" you need to generate revenue. I know it sounds simple, but it is very uncommon! A new entrepreneur will see Twitter or Facebook start without making any money and assume that it's okay to do that. These are the rare exceptions, but for the majority of businesses it's not okay to not produce revenue. The reality is, we all need money to survive and therefore it is a key requirement that a business generates revenue. It is also not good enough to simply have a general idea of how a business will make money.

This is the most critical piece of your Square Business Plan! Without this, you will not bring in any money, even if you have the best product in the world!

I wanted to know if there were any key distinctions between a millionaire's business model. Where there certain ones that worked better than others?

The revenue models vary. But one key distinction is that they are scalable, and almost all of them have an online component, or a huge distribution network. Many of them also have more than one business now, so they have taken what they learned and leveraged that into other businesses and industries.

Table 6.2 is a list of some millionaires and what their businesses sell. This will help you get a few ideas on what is working well for them.

Entrance/Launch Strategy

You need to know how to reach your customers as you go into business. There is a big difference between sales and marketing. Sales is going out and finding your customers and selling to them. Marketing is the act of promoting your business, with the intention that interested parties come to you.

At the beginning stages you want your strategy to be the fastest way to the money. You want to make sure that you are generating revenue as soon as possible.

Millionaires advocate knowing how to sell. Your product or service might be so amazing that everyone will want it, and you don't have to do much selling. But most of the time, you need to know how to sell.

On the other hand, millionaires also advocate testing to see what works in marketing/advertising. Unfortunately, you don't know exactly what your market will respond to. A few ideas to help you choose the right strategies to test are:

- How is your competition advertising?
- How much money do you have to spend? (This makes a huge difference, because if you don't have a lot, you will probably be choosing Facebook ads instead of TV ads.)
- Where does your market see advertisements?

A Millionaire's First Month in Business

So what does the first month in business look like for a millionaire? Here are two examples of what the first month in business looked like for two different businesses. One is a product-based business, and the other is service-based. You'll notice the continuous forward motion toward the goal.

Table 6.2   Millionaires and Their Businesses

Millionaire	Business	Business Description
Brad Schy	Musical Chairs	Sells tickets to great seats at events (musicals, basketball games, concerts); helps people find coveted seats
Andrew Darbyshire	Pacsoft	Produces software for lumber- and hardware stores
Craig Wolfe	CelebriDucks	Manufactures and sells rubber ducks that look like celebrities
Hanny Lerner	MOD Restoration	Furniture reupholstery
Ryan Eldridge	Nerds On Call	Computer/network servicing
Ken Wisnefski	WebiMax	Manages online marketing, SEO, social media of companies
David Hirschkop	Dave's Gourmet	Manufactures and sells sauces and condiments (specialty: hot sauces, particularly Dave's Insanity Hot Sauce)
Linda Stanfield	Ben Franklin the Punctual Plumber	Plumbing service
Marissa Levin	Information Experts	Provides strategic marketing, education and training, human capital, interactive website design and development, conference planning—a whole host of strategic communications services

Anita Crook, founder of Pouchee, on the first month:

I had ordered 2,000 of them manufactured. I didn't know if anybody else would like them or not, but I took a chance and it turned out that people really did like it. I started showing them, when I got my first samples in. I went from store to store and I thought a really cool place to sell these would be in boutiques and gift boutiques so I went to some local places that I thought were really cute places and showed them my little

Pouchee and they loved it and they bought them. Within the first month, I was sold out.

It was phenomenal because anybody who knows me knows I am not a salesperson. I was scared to death to go into my first store and actually try to sell them something, especially something that I had produced. I don't take rejection well so I was really afraid I was going to run out of the store crying, if they had not liked it.

I was petrified while trying to sell my first one. My knees were shaking. I really almost had a panic attack. I really did. I just had to take a deep breath and pray and just seek divine help to get through that first door. It was kind of a funny situation because I walked in, you know, and I am showing my little Pouchee and it was the mother and daughter situation, the daughter owned the store, I think her mother helped her out. The daughter looked at them and she said, "You know, I just bought these other things" and it was a totally different kind of concept. She had just bought some and she said, "I just bought these, when I sell out of these, I'll look at yours." I'm going okay, can I show it to you anyway and she said, "Sure."

Her mother was standing there and then the daughter went to help a customer and the mother came back. She said, "I really like yours. Can I buy one?" I said, "Sure, I'll even give you the wholesale price because I think you'll buy more." As it turned out, before I left the store, the daughter was onboard and she bought a whole order.

Bobby Casey, of Global Wealth Protection, on the first month of his first business, which put together bicycles for large chain stores:

I must have visited 60 Walmarts driving all over North Carolina and Virginia. Literally driving to the store, walking to the office and asking to speak to the store manager and just asking him straight up would you be interested in hiring me as your contract bike assembler. Finally I found one store in Durham, North Carolina, that took me in and helped me get started and this and that.

It was at least 60 stores I went to before I finally found one that said, "Yeah, yeah, okay we'll hire you, how much do you charge?"

At the time, I basically had no money. I had a negative net worth at that time and I think I might have also had a negative income as well. I racked up a bunch of credit card debt just driving around to stores. Just paying for gas, filling up your gas tank, driving around for several weeks at a time—no, no, no, no.

But I wouldn't have stopped if it took me 300 stores.

In both cases they were new entrepreneurs. In both cases they didn't let excuses stop them. They pushed through the fear, through the tough times, through the negative thoughts to *make* their companies successful. Many times it's the entrepreneur who makes the business, not just the product! (If Bobby had given up after 50 stores, no one could say he didn't try. But he also wouldn't have had a multimillion-dollar business.)

Marketing versus Sales

Let's define the difference between marketing and sales a bit more. **Marketing** is just where you reach your prospect and try to persuade them to purchase your product or service. **Sales** is where you are actually asking for your prospect to buy your product. You could market a ton and not actually get any sales. Sales is the most important piece of your business because that is where the revenue is generated from, but it's a double-edged sword, if you don't have prospects to ask to buy then you don't have sales either!

When you are planning your launch strategy you want to include both marketing and sales. First you want to figure out how to sell to your customers. You learned a ton about what your customers want in Chapter 4. Now you can figure out how to specifically sell to them.

Once you learn what they respond to when it comes to sales then you can start to turn up that firehouse of prospects and market to them.

Selling That Works

No one likes the used car dealer sales type. Think about it, you would never want to be pushed into a sale.

I *hated* sales. I thought there was only one type of selling, unethical. What I didn't realize is that there is an amazing and very ethical way to sell. I can sum in up in three words:

Help Your Customers.

It's not about you. It's about making your customers' lives better. It has to make sense for them and for you. If it's a win-win, then you are doing it right.

I worked at a place that sold high-end vacuum cleaners when I was younger and was taught some unethical selling techniques, so I just assumed all sales wasn't good. That experience severely limited me when I got into business. I had to relearn sales. Once

I did, it changed the way I did business (and the money I made!). So I highly recommend investing time in learning how to sell. You can always hire better salespeople than you as you grow, but most of the time, the owner does a lot of selling as you are starting up!

Neil Patel, Founder of KISSmetrics and serial entrepreneur, worked for that same company I did selling high-end vacuum cleaners. Learn what he thinks about selling people what they want:

> I lived in Orange County and I didn't grow up in the richest part of Orange County. So selling vacuums to an area when the average person only makes $30,000 a year when the vacuum costs like $2,000 isn't that doable.
>
> Once I realized and I know this is kind of bad, that most people wouldn't buy vacuums from me but I realized they liked the cleaning and they would pay for it, because people were like "could you clean the other room," I started charging them to clean more rooms in their house.
>
> If I sell the vacuum I make about a $100 in commission and I couldn't sell one a day. If I sold one in a week I'd be lucky but I would make more consistent money and more if I charged to clean each and every single room. Same amount of work.

Instead of his trying to convince someone to buy something they couldn't afford, he instead sold them something they actually wanted and could afford! This is the essence of ethical marketing.

The Sales Pitch

Many larger or more expensive products and services need a sales pitch. If you are selling a $10,000 website, usually your customer will need to talk to you before they plunk down a check!

Yet if you are a web developer just starting your own company, you may have never sold anything before. There is an art to sales that comes as you do it more and more. Here are a few tips and stories.

Tips from Neil Patel, owner of KISSmetrics and serial entrepreneur

Tip #1: You need to practice to get better at sales!

I would still try and step in there and try to persuade them as to why I should clean their homes, I'd have different sales pitches and I would try different ones out. I would even offer them a knife set all the time even after they said no and I would try to persuade them.

Tip #2: Give your customer what they want.

It's all about figuring out what problems people have when you're selling, what their budget is, and giving them the simplest solution that makes them interested. Don't start by telling them how you're going to solve their problems and all the benefits.

Don't say, "Here is how I am going to solve this and blah, blah."

Ask them about their problems first. Get deep into learning about their problem and understanding what worked and didn't work for them. Then sell the benefits that you know will help.

Tip #3: Scarcity works very well.

Scarcity is when something is in short supply. It's a simple tactic that is proven over and over again to work. Look at eBay! The timed auctions make people hunt and snap up items over and over again.

You create a scarcity by saying something like "Hey I only have one opening left" or "Hey if you sign up now we can start in the next week but if you don't sign up now we're going to have to wait 30 days to sign up or to get started because of XYZ reason."

Bonus Tip: Sell Money, from Jeffrey Fox, bestselling author and founder of Fox and Company

Jeffrey Fox is a sales expert and explains his best sales tactic, which he calls "Dollarization." In essence it's finding out how much the problem is costing your potential customers and putting it into numbers. That way they can clearly see the benefit of what they are buying.

> What we do and what the great companies do, every advertising claim, no matter what it is can be dollarized. If you're claim is your products last longer, are faster, lighter, quieter, whatever, you can turn that claim into numbers. If you can make the claim that we last longer, then what are the facts? Our product lasts two years, the other guy lasts one year. That's a fact. Well, then you can dollarize that difference and that's what we do for clients all over the world.
>
> Our clients sell money. When we're done with them, they aren't selling mass spectrometers, they're selling 10 freed-up days of a pharmaceutical laboratory and each freed-up day is worth a million dollars so when the customer gives our guy $450,000 for a mass spectrometer, our guy in turn gives that customer 10 free days of laboratory time or $10 million. So, $10 million minus $450,000 is $9,550,000. That's the return on

investment a big farmer gets from investing in our client's mass spectrometer. You can do that for every single product.

And for new products, if the dollarized value is in fact not as good as the prevailing pricing of the competition, then you don't launch the new product. If you dollarize the value of your product and services to XYZ company and you cannot show the company a true dollarized value proposition, a positive return on investment in your product or service, then you don't sell to that company. You sell somewhere else. So, in tough times, he or she who sells money has a distinct advantage over he or she who is selling a product asking for money.

The most important question in business is: If I were the customer, knowing what I know about the customer, the competition, the marketplace, if I were the customer, me the salesperson, why would I do business with me?

And if they can answer that question honestly, objectively, hard-headedly, hopefully in terms of dollars and cents, then they have an ironclad platform for making the deal.

There are many sales tactics out there, but just concentrate on these four right now. The next time you chat with your avatar, invite him or her to sit down and chat more. Then use the template that follows to get the sales conversation going. Practice as much as you possibly can!

Sales Pitch Template

Every business needs a good system to follow to produce sales. You don't want to reinvent the wheel each time. Follow these four steps to create your sales pitch.

1. Get comfortable.

You want to create an environment that isn't salesy. Ideally you want to come out of this interaction friends, whether they buy or not. Try to find something to connect with them on—if you both have children the same age, similar hobbies, and so on.

Then let them know how these conversations usually go. Be clear on what will be going on, and how long it will take; that way you are both working under the same expectations.

You might say something like, "Do we still have about 40 minutes, does that still work for you?" (Prospect says yes.)

"Perfect. Well, just so you know how this normally works, I am going to have a ton of questions for you, I really want to determine what you really need to see if this might be a fit. You can ask me whatever questions you have too of course!"

2. Ask questions, find out what they need.

Don't pitch, just ask. The potential customers should be doing more of the talking than you. You can't solve a problem that they have if you aren't clear on exactly what that problem is. Asking questions, and getting more information is the easiest way to find out about what they need and if it lines up with what you have to offer.

Questions like:

What isn't working well right now?

What are you doing to fix the problem?

What have you done in the past to fix it, and did it work? Tell me more about that. What is that costing you (in time or money)?

3. Use that information to dollarize, and find a win-win situation.

Use the information you already received and try to put numbers to it. If you know that they will save a specific amount of money, or time, show them clearly how the math works out. The numbers make it a concrete reason—instead of telling the prospect about how it's a better value, give them numbers that show them.

4. Ask them to buy.

If you are not used to selling, or are scared, it can be hard to ask for the sale. This is critical, though! Many sales are lost even if the customer is interested because this last piece was missing.

Ways to ask for the sale:

Would it make sense to work together? Or, Are you interested in moving forward on this?

If it doesn't make sense for them to buy it, don't try and sell it! That's why we think of used car salespeople as sleazy. The stereo typical used car salesperson is trying to sell us into anything, no matter what we need! If it doesn't fit, try to recommend something else that does. Even make a recommendation or intro to someone else you know who might be a better fit. Your prospect will clearly see your integrity.

Marketing

I've tried to nail down specific marketing tactics that work for the millionaires' businesses. But they usually respond with the same answer:

It depends on the business.

Serial entrepreneurs know that a marketing tactic that works in one industry doesn't necessarily work in another, or even in the same industry. There are too many variables. Marketing is not a one-size-fits-all solution. Facebook marketing might work wonders for some businesses, while print catalogs work for others.

Even if it seems like your business might be a perfect fit for Facebook marketing, it still might not work.

So how can you find out what does work?

We can get a good general idea on things to test by taking these four steps:

Step 1: Look at competitors in your industry.

Usually if people are spending money on it consistently, it's working. (Unless the business has no idea what it is doing!)

Chat with your avatar to learn where they find other companies like yours. Are they looking online, or are they asking for recommendations from their friends?

Step 2: Look for current possible strategies that might work for your industry.

Listen to podcasts, or read blogs or books to find out what might have worked in the past for your specific industry.

Step 3: Choose the most likely options.

This depends on your business and budget, so I suggest that you write a list and then rank your options so you know which to test first. Use the following worksheet.

Marketing Tactic	Estimated Cost to Test	Rank

Step 4: Marketing test strategy.

Most small businesses tend to not be very good at tracking things, which means that a lot of effort is wasted, and we don't have true results.

Who knows if your radio ad worked unless you track it?

I have seen businesses drop thousands of dollars on an ad, and barely get the gist of whether it is working. I spoke to one person about the success of a previous radio ad and he tried to remember if the phone rang more that week or not. Be diligent about tracking results to your marketing campaigns.

Track results based on whatever your metrics are and KPIs that you chose in your Square Business Plan.

The following example shows you tracking with Revenue Generated.

These are *very* simple spreadsheets because we just need something simple that will actually be used.

Marketing Tactic	Cost	Revenue Generated

You need to track what marketing tactic brings in what revenue. If it's a newspaper ad, you'll need to make sure your employees are asking customers where they heard about you. If you have coupons or deals online make sure you track where they come from. The tracking is the annoying part, but it's the part that really matters.

Marketing Ideas

Here is a list of marketing strategies to get you started with your testing.

Online Marketing Strategies

Facebook Ads
Facebook (Organic)
YouTube (and Ads)
Twitter
Google+
Pinterest
Pay Per Click
Banner Ads
E-Mail Marketing
Search Engine Optimization (SEO)
Blogging
Podcasting
Interactive Tools
Mobile Apps
Digital Magazines (iPad Magazines)
Webinars/Teleseminars
Sponsorships
Daily Deal Sites
Joint Ventures
Viral Video
Online PR
Craigslist
Directory Listings

Offline Marketing Strategies

Direct Mail
Cold Calling
Brochures
Business Cards
Networking Events
Guerrilla Marketing
Promotional Materials
Business Associations
Billboards
Radio Advertising
Print Media Ads
Referrals

Hanny Lerner Launched Her Company Using a Groupon

Actually, our biggest break when it came to reupholstery was that I contacted Groupon and I said, "Hey we want to make a Groupon deal," and this was before we had any reupholstery clients. They said, "Okay, well tell us what you got." I said, "Reupholstery, get $200 for $95." I don't even know if we carried fabrics then, but I said fabrics. We sold 95 Groupons and that was what kick-started our upholstery business. We suddenly went from zero to 95 clients overnight. It changed our life.

The day it went live, we knew that the phones were going to be ringing off the hook because even if your deal isn't so great, there are still a million people calling you about your deal. So we brought in some friends to sit in on the phones.

Suddenly, the phone was ringing off the hook, people had questions, and we figured once the Groupon thing was over, we'd figure out how to do the work. We didn't actually do upholstery work at that point. It was a three-day deal, so for the first three days it was just about getting people to buy. I couldn't say that we were mavens in upholstery. We were literally learning as we went. And people bought.

Each marketing experience will be different, but keep pushing forward. Keep testing to see what your market wants and how they want to learn about your product.

Action Item: Fill Out the Launch Strategy Template Below

Your Launch Strategy Template

Sales

How many do you need to sell the first month? Consider factors such as how much money it takes to produce your good/service, and cost or employees.

How many sales appointments do you need to have before you sell one?

How many prospects do you need to speak with to get a sales appointment?

How many prospects do you need to engage with each week to hit your sales numbers?

Total Revenue Needed

Marketing Ideas and Budget

1. _____
2. _____
3. _____
4. _____
5. _____

6. _____
7. _____
8. _____
9. _____
10. _____

Market Testing

Marketing Tactic	Cost	Revenue Generated

Top Three Marketing Strategies

1. _____
2. _____
3. _____

Launch Action Plan

Month One:

Month Two:

Month Three:

Resources

Don't take for granted the resources you already have at your disposal. Some millionaires already had amazing networks within their industry before they left. Others had no network at all. Consider the following:

Access to Prospects

Melanie Duncan, who owns a variety of businesses online and also hosts a podcast, had an amazing resource. She was part of a sorority that led her to find her need, but it also gave her access to many college students, her perfect target market!

Network

Influence & Co.'s founder John Hall had an amazing network of journalists and people in the media and online.

Skills

Michael Port started as an actor, so he had amazing skills in speaking and being charismatic.

Marissa Levin had all of the knowledge from her previous job to start her own business, plus she had amazing sales skills.

Advice

Frank McKinney had access to many wealth clients with his tennis business, and he started talking to them and gaining advice.

Time

Serial entrepreneur Aaron Pitman was young, and didn't know much about business, but he had time on his side. He didn't have many expenses, and he was able to dedicate a lot of time trying things to see if they worked.

You might also realize the resources that you might *need* as you go through this. This is very important, because there might be gaping holes in what you are missing in your business. This is where we find those holes. Do you have no way of reaching prospects? Or is time a limiting factor for you? What is missing that you can find before you start?

Do I Need Funding?

Do you need funding? Most of the time, the millionaires bootstrapped their businesses, which just means that they didn't take any funding and tried to make the business profitable as soon as possible.

There are many types of funding that this book won't get into. If you want a direction to start, look up angel funding. Angel funding is usually a smaller amount that you get at the beginning of your business to start it off well.

Many of the people I interview are angel investors, which means they seek to give angel funding to people starting up new businesses. I think we can learn a lot from what they are looking for in the businesses they invest in. It helps you understand what makes a viable company. Even if you don't want to get funding, this is important info.

Aaron Pitman—How He Picks Angel Investments

If a potential startup is aggressive and they're into the idea and you can just feel that they're passionate about it, I'll listen and I will build a relationship with that person.

I invest in whatever I feel like is actually going to make money. I don't want to invest $20,000 to make $40,000 because I can do that in my own business. I want to invest 20, 40, 50, $100,000 because I know I can make 10, 20, 30 times my money. I invest in home runs. You have to have the mentality that you're going to hit a home run. If they have the mentality and their business idea makes sense, I'll give it a whirl.

Square Business Plan Done

Take this one piece at a time. It might even take you a month to implement this entire chapter. But proper planning, questioning, and testing will lay the foundation to a strong business!

The end result you will have is a strong sense of exactly who is willing to buy your product or service, how you are going to reach them, and how you will take in money. You might run into road-blocks. You might not be sure what is going to work or not. Things will be uncertain.

But you will grow as a person and business owner as you implement this. You will get past your excuses and learn a ton. Do the work and keep going and you will make your first sale. The sweetness of your first sale is amazing!

ACTION ITEM REVIEW

Action Item: Square Business Plan

Table 6.1   Square Business Plans

Mission Statement	USP/Key Differentiator
Avatar	Resources Available

Business Metric	Launch Strategy
Metric #1	#1
Metric #2	#2
Metric #3	#3

Download the Square Business Plan at http://EventualMillionaire.com.

Action Item

Brainstorm your why. Then write down many ideas for how it helps people.

Start to play with possible mission statements. Write down 5 to 10 and see which ones resonate most strongly with your gut feeling.

Action Item

Choose three performance indicators to start measuring in this new company. If you have an online e-commerce company, it might be visitors, conversion rates, and revenue.

_____

_____

_____

_____

_____

_____

_____

_____

Action Item: Fill Out the Launch Strategy Template Below

Your Launch Strategy Template

Sales

How many do you need to sell the first month? Consider factors such as how much money it takes to produce your good/service, and cost or employees.

How many sales appointments do you need to do before you sell one?

How many prospects do you need to talk to get a sales appointment?

How many prospects do you need to engage with each week to hit your sales numbers?

Total Revenue Needed

Marketing Ideas and Budget

1. _____
2. _____
3. _____
4. _____
5. _____

6. _____
7. _____
8. _____
9. _____
10. _____

Market Testing

Marketing Tactic	Cost	Revenue Generated

Top Three Marketing Strategies

1. _____
2. _____
3. _____

Launch Action Plan

Month One:

Month Two:

Month Three:

CHAPTER 7

Your Success Is a Series of Small Wins

Success is the progressive realization of worthwhile goals and dreams.

—Paul Meyer

We've all enjoyed success in life. It can range from finishing a college degree to paying off a credit card. It can even be deciding that you will be a millionaire and taking that first action toward that goal. It all adds up to the life you are living now.

I know the typical eventual millionaire is a high achiever and high achievers feel really good when they are realizing their goals. I'm willing to bet you have set goals before. I wanted to find out how exactly millionaires set their goals, and not just how they set them, but what they did with them after they were set. I want to show you how millionaires go through and set their visions and their goals. You'll learn if visioning and goal setting is just another self-help thing people say that may or may not work, or if it's really working for the successful.

After asking millionaires how they set up their goals, it was clear to see that they do similar things, like visioning and creating specific goals and action plans. All individuals are different and have their own way of doing things. You can still be successful even without setting goals, but the majority of the millionaires I've spent time with have goals.

Why Visioning Is Important to Millionaires

If you want to be an entrepreneur, you already have a key feature: you have a vision that no one else has. You dream of bigger and better things for this world.

Vonda White, CEO of Collegiate Risk Management and success coach, summed it up when she said, "I want to encourage people to dream big and to take a risk, because life is exciting. It has so much to offer, but it's up to us to decide will we step out there and take that risk." So this is where you decide on that dream.

Before I ever started interviewing millionaires I wondered if millionaires used visioning. Was it too "out there"? It doesn't seem very scientific, but I had heard gurus suggest it over and over and I wondered if there was something to it.

After interviewing about 10 different people it started to become clear. Millionaires used visioning. Now, after more than 100 interviews, it shines like a beacon.

They use it to their advantage often.

Do you? If you don't have a vision, you are missing out on a critical piece.

Now, if you don't have a vision, you might be wandering around for a long time. It's like stopping at every destination to decide if this is the place you want to end up. If your goal is to get to Fiji, but you don't know what Fiji will look like until you see it, you will end up stopping at many destinations and looking around to see if it is the right place. You'll get to Fiji eventually, but it might take a very long time.

Adrian John Cartwood, a personal finance blogger who started 7million7years.com, said, "I boil it down not to luck or intelligence as most people think, or even the Midas touch. I boil it down to having a vision, where you actually have to get out a certain financial result. Once people have something to do, it's amazing how good they are at doing it."

According to Joyce Schwarz, author of *The Vision Board*, "Visioning is an ancient art and science that dates back to the caveman days, which is a combination of meditation, soul-searching, and even improv."

It's imagining and feeling what the future looks like. You want to harness those thoughts into a crystal-clear vision of your future with as much detail as possible. Then you can refer to that same vision over and over again. I think you should blend both your personal and business vision. We are only one person with different pieces, and we should address all of those pieces! Include your family, friends, lifestyle, finances, and business in your vision.

If that vision includes a million dollars, why? What do you think that would do for you?

Does that create a feeling for you? Or a specific lifestyle? Does it allow you to give more, or feel more secure?

Michael Stelzner, from SocialMediaExaminer.com, said, "Say to yourself where do I want to be in five years and write it down with a pen and write out as much detail as you can. What I want you to do next is ask this question, act like you've already been there and you've achieved it in five years, say, 'What did I do just before I achieved it?' Let's say the goal is to become a millionaire or let's say the goal is to have a *New York Times* best seller or whatever. What did I do just a month before that happened? Let's say it was this. Let's say it was got on *Oprah,* I don't know. What did I do to get on *Oprah?* Just start working all the way back to the present and guess what you'll have—a map!"

Michael Stelzner, a serial entrepreneur himself, had some amazing questions to ask yourself when you are just starting to set up your vision for your business.

Visioning: Business Questions to Ask

What do I want to achieve?
Where do I want to go?
Why do I want it?
What are my underlying motivations?
Can others rally around the vision?
What perceived problems am I addressing?
What will it look like once I have accomplished it?

Here are a few other questions to ask:

Visioning: Personal Questions to Ask

Where do I live?
What does my family look like?
What does a typical day look like?
How's my health?

How much money do I earn each year?
What are some amazing things that I have accomplished?
What lifestyle do I live?
What things have I learned?

There are three things to think about when you are creating your personal vision: there are things you can have, things you can do, and things you can be. Think about all three when creating your vision.

The End Game

No one wants his or her end game to be working 60 or more hours per week—not even millionaires, even if they love their work. You need to figure out your end game, though that doesn't mean to know what you want to do until you are 80. We can have multiple end games. We just need to figure out what our first vision is now.

Millionaire Derek Sivers, founder and former president of CD Baby, suggests this exercise: Think of yourself as 90 years old looking back at your life. Let's say you're 30 and you have 10 different things you want to be doing. You might think that you can't get anything done! You *can* actually do them all—it's just that you have to be patient and do them sequentially. Remember the donkey from Chapter 4? Visioning is a way to bring focus to your outlook for the future.

Have Fun with It

Visioning can be a fun experience. Once you have the vision, you can bring it up whenever you want. When you have a very tough day, and you think, "Why am I doing all of this?" that's when you let the amazing experience of achieving your goals play out in your mind.

Many people like to watch TV to escape their feelings of their day, but they are feeding their minds with things that are mostly negative. Think about the TV or movies you watch. How many of them are positive and make you feel uplifted? Most movies now are based on suspense or violence.

Use Visioning to Make Decisions

You can use visioning to make decisions. You're going to face many decisions in your life and business. Use your vision as a guide and ask yourself if I were that person in my vision now, what decision would I make? What is the best decision in this situation that would get me to that vision?

Use Your Heart

JV Crum III, CEO of Conscious Millionaire Institute, said:

> One of the real secrets is having your heart fully in it. Is your heart in it? That is so critical. If it's just a mental thing with you, that's the problem with most people's visualizations. They're talking about focusing your mind. Yeah, big deal, but focus your heart, bigger deal. Then your body has got to be just in this ready state of action to move you forward and you're only taking actions that are going to lead one after another exactly to that result and anything that's not getting you there, just keep being conscious. It's an iterative process.

What does your heart think? What does your gut think? You can sit in your head all day long, but true success comes from you as a whole person. So does visualization.

Action Item

Create Your Vision

Step 1: The Future of Your Creating a Vision Is Experiencing What Your Life Will Be Like Long Term. Think about Yourself 10 Years or Even 20 Years in the Future

Who are you in your vision? Are you confident and conquering the world? Is that how you act now? Write a list of 10 characteristics that describe you in the future.

1. _____	6. _____
2. _____	7. _____
3. _____	8. _____
4. _____	9. _____
5. _____	10. _____

If you are having a hard time with this, find someone you respect now, who embodies the characteristics you want and write those down.

You can use these characteristics to grow. Daily work on each of these characteristics will move you forward fast. You can make amazing changes in a year to become the person that runs the company and the life you want.

Step 2: The Future of Your Business, Think about Your Business Long Term

- Where is the industry going? Will you be on the cutting edge?
- What has your business done in the past 10 or 20 years that has made it remarkable?

This will help you be ahead of the curve in your business, and we will also work with these in the next module.

Step 3: Sum It Up!

Think about your life in 10 years. What do you want your life personally and professionally to look like?

Visioning with Meditation

A few of the interviewees have mentioned that they use meditation as a way to practice and remind them of their vision.

Millionaire interviewee Amy Applebaum (Amyapplebaum.com) is not only an amazing success coach, she also has dozens of hypno-therapy CDs. She actually created a new company using her skills in hypnotherapy:

> The reason I got certified was not to have a hypnotherapy practice, it was to learn more about how our mind works and how we can have a good mind-set and all of those things that you need to be successful in business. So, I've been using the education that I received from that for years but I never did anything with it until recently when I was looking for new opportunities in my business to help support people in becoming successful. And what I mind in the female entrepreneur marketplace is a lot of doubts, a lot of interesting conversations around money and the fear of making money, and confidence

issues yet there are so many female entrepreneurs stampeding the entrepreneurial marketplace. So, I thought to myself this is the time to bring the hypnotherapy stuff out. Success is really about two things in order to achieve it: how you think and what you do. And in business coaching, I've been addressing what you need to do for all these years. Of course, peppered in there is mind-set but I hadn't dedicated products to how do you think and the type of thinking you need to be successful, this was going to be my opportunity to do that.

Free gift: Amy is giving you a download of one of her hypnotherapy meditation CDs all about visioning. I use it often and love it!
Go to http://EventualMillionaire.com/BookBonus to download.

Referencing Your Vision

It's not only about creating that vision, but about *using* that vision. That means bringing it up during your meditations, or rereading it often. It may also mean creating a drawing or vision board that you put up on your wall.

What can you put in place that will make you go back to it often? It should be *fun* to revisit and fun to daydream about your amazing future.

Action Item

Do the exercises and create your crystal-clear vision. Then create your crystal-clear vision in just a few sentences. Write it down and create your goals based on it.

How Millionaires Set and Attain Their Goals

It's amazing how many millionaires use the word *goal* in their language. My main **goal** was the original **goal**, that's a great **goal** to have. Even when millionaires are speaking about being kids, they all had goals. Goals are a huge part of their lives.

But setting goals isn't the hard part. It's all that other stuff that's hard—keeping up with them, remembering to focus, and making decisions based on them.

To successfully achieve our vision, first we are going to set the goal, but we are going to set it *knowing* that we need to set up the processes that will remind us to focus on them in our daily lives. It's more detailed than the typical SMART goals. Todd Tresidder of FinancialMentor.com, said, "You only want to work off what you can actually achieve within a confined time frame, otherwise you drop into overwhelm."

Tony Hartl, founder of Planet Tan, sets goals like this:

My annual goals are broken out by personal, business, and family. Within each of those categories, they can be as little as four or five up to maybe seven and then what happens is I have what's called a *Gantt chart*. Now this is a little sophisticated because of my assistant and she's a business intelligence person so she creates deadlines for every one of my goals but I set up goals within those categories and every month I review my goals and that's why I think I have such a high level of success of hitting my goals because they're in my face all the time.

You've got to create personal accountability. If you're not reviewing your goals on a month-in, month-out basis, and here's the benefit once you do it. Then you can go back and look at 2008 and say what did I say I was going to do and when a year goes by, you should be able to say hey did I become a better person? Did I achieve something? Did I make a difference in my community? The world? Personally? Did I learn a language? Whatever it is. Did I qualify for the Boston marathon? Whatever it is. Then you should be able to go back and go oh yeah, 2010 rocked. I got my sailing license, I qualified for Boston, I achieved this much in income, I sold this many books, whatever it is.

You should be able to review that and then what you do is you put those annual, you print out that sheet once the year is over and you put it in a file and I have every one of my one-year goals and I review that.

And Guy Kawasaki, best-selling author and venture capitalist, said:

Well, I mean this might not be so popular an answer, but I don't think the goal should be to make a million dollars.

I think the goal should be to make the world a better place, increase people's creativity or productivity and I think that making a million dollars is a natural outcome of successfully changing the world. So the way it works is you focus on changing the world, you'll probably make a million dollars. If you focus on making a million dollars, you might make a million dollars but I think you'll probably be less successful. Don't focus on the reward, focus on the goal.

Everyone I've asked about goals said something similar to what Vonda White says:

When I have a goal I've written it down and then I know I need to make this happen to achieve the goal. What my action steps are for today, tomorrow, this week, next week, for this whole month, and so on.

I also heard stories of before they found success. Did they set goals then? Most of the time they referenced drifting and having no goals, like this quote from Adrian John Cartwood:

I had no goals and every day was "As long as I'm not broke I'll keep going." I paid myself a small wage and I could eat. That was it.

So millionaires have had their down times, too. But it seems like during their up times it was all because of goal setting and it has been said that a goal is just a dream with a date on it.

So we've been banged over the head so many times on how important goals are, but, in my experience working directly with business owners and setting their goals, I know most of us could improve not only how we set goals but how we work on our goals. Let's help you not only set goals but actually stick with them and achieve them.

Setting the Goal

Each millionaire has a slightly different way of setting their goals but they all accomplish the same objectives. First they set the goal. They put it somewhere where they will see it and they have a system to review it, either monthly or by having someone there for accountability. Then they only focus on the next step.

Pick one main goal. We get *way* too caught up in wanting everything now. Yes, I want everything now, too! But if we don't put a laser focus on our goals, we will water things down. Choose only one focus for your business, for now. To pick that one goal, you need to first figure out the priorities in your business.

Priorities   What is the number one most important thing in your business? What are numbers two and three?

If you don't know what is most important in your business, you cannot effectively make decisions about the year ahead. Is customer retention the biggest factor in your success? Is it improving conversions on your online campaigns?

Once you have chosen the one goal that describes your year, answer these questions:

> How would you feel in 5, 10, or 20 years if you never reached this goal?
> Is it bold enough?
> Do you believe you can achieve it?
> Does this conflict with any other goals?
> What obstacles will be in your way?
> What people or groups will you need to work with to achieve the goal?
> What knowledge will you need to complete this goal?
> Are you 100 percent committed?
> What are the benefits of achieving it? What pain will there be if you don't achieve it?

After you answer these questions, you should have a general feeling if this goal is big enough to be scary, hard enough to matter, and exciting enough to really commit to—no matter what. If you don't feel strongly enough about your goal, change it.

The COVENANT Framework for Goal Setting

When I started looking at the data and tools that millionaires used, many of them used the SMART goal-setting framework.

SMART stands for:

- Specific
- Measurable

- Attainable
- Realistic
- Time

It's more than just setting a goal that says, "I want more money this year." It's making it concrete with numbers and a time frame. But I found that there are a few key pieces that the millionaires have done, which aren't included on the SMART goals.

Millionaires ask themselves questions like, "Who is going to keep me accountable for this goal?" or "Does this goal align with my values?" (If you don't think it's all about the money, yet your goal is solely money-focused, that might not make for a happy life!)

Those pieces are missing from the SMART system, and both are critical to make sure you achieve them.

Instead I created the COVENANT framework. First, Merriam-Webster says a covenant is "a formal, solemn, and binding agreement." When you set a goal, you create a pact, something deeper than a goal that is forgotten in a journal or on your computer.

Take goal setting seriously. Don't let this be another goal you set and never look at again.

COVENANT stands for:

- Commitment
- Organized
- Values/Vision
- Enlightened
- Noticeable
- Accountability
- Numerical
- Time

Commitment You really need to be dedicated to your goal. It's more than a wish or a hope—it's a real pledge to yourself. So how committed are you to your goal? Let's say you were to work extremely hard for three months straight, but you don't see any progress. Or maybe you only see a little bit of progress, but it isn't really what you hoped for. You're disheartened, and friends and family are telling you to give it up and just move on. Would you give it up?

Would you stop working toward your goal just because of all these circumstances, or do you really, really want it? If you would give up, then this might be a goal that is really great for a little while and then peters off toward the end because you can't sustain it. This question is really just a check-in to yourself to make sure you're really dedicated.

Frank McKinney said this about committing when he was referring to training for the Badwater Ultramarathon:

> Friday night, I went out to train sleep deprived. I worked all week, I worked on Friday. Friday at 9 P.M. I started running and I ran until 7 in the morning, until the sun came up.
>
> There's moments where I'm like, "Why am I doing this?" Everybody goes to sleep but I have other things I have to do. So when it comes to preparing the mind and the body for something like that, going back to our one, having that coach who sat me down, it was more of an Internet relationship than a direct relationship, where she would send me a schedule of a workout schedule, a training schedule for the week and I adhered to it, every single thing she told me to do I did. When it came to running and cross-training and the proper diet and so I really converted myself.
>
> I was a casual six-mile-every-other-day runner and I really found, not found a way, but I believed there was a way to convert myself from that casual one step from being a couch potato kind of person to being an ultramarathoner. Now after five, going on the sixth year, I'm an expert.

Organized   Being organized is a recurring theme with millionaires when it comes to reaching their goals. How can you break your goal down into organized and manageable chunks? Being organized means that everyone knows what the goal of the company is. They know what systems need to be created to get there. This is especially important for long-term goals. Break them down into short-term goals and organize what needs to be accomplished for each. It should act like a map, where you consistently look at what you need to do for the next few steps. That way you can do something tangible with your goal and only focus on the next logical step.

Values/Vision   Your goal really needs to fit the rest of your life and your vision for the future. If your number-one priority is your family, but your goal requires you to work 80 hours per week, then the goal doesn't align with your vision or values. Compare your vision that you just created and your goal. Do they seem to align?

Enlightened Being selfish with your goals is okay. To take your goals to the next level, however, you can have what you want but also help others in the process, and that's when your goal becomes enlightened. It's helping others while you help yourself, just like that great Zig Ziglar quote, "You can have everything in life you want if you will just help enough other people get what they want."

Most Eventual Millionaires that I survey want to be financially free so they can help others. You can do that now even before you become a millionaire. Let's incorporate being enlightened into your goal now. How can this goal that you already have help others in the process? For example, maybe you do want to hit your revenue goals because you plan on giving back, or you want to hire two key employees—not only to help your business but also to provide them with an amazing place to work, financial stability, and maybe flexibility for them and their family. It really then becomes a win-win situation.

Noticeable Your goal needs to be seen.

Once it's complete, print it out, and put it where you will notice it every single day. Tony Hartl had a chart in his office. Frank McKinney had it on his laptop. You can put it on your refrigerator, whiteboard, bedside table—anywhere that you will see it every single day.

Accountability The point of this step is to set up the system of accountability in advance. I know that some people feel that if they don't have the drive and willpower to push through their goals themselves, then they don't deserve it or they don't want it enough. But everyone, even millionaires, need accountability and support, and they need to be reminded and pushed sometimes, too. That's why accountability is so important.

This means setting up and committing to the mastermind group to be accountable to your goals. Or this means finding a good friend with whom you can be "accountability buddies." This is a key piece and where most goal setting fails.

Numerical Your goal needs to have measurements to gauge your progress. You may have already created your KPIs (key performance indicators) in your business plan. You can measure these now to see your progress as it goes and, at the end, you will know whether you've achieved that goal if you hit that right number. It can be revenue, conversion rate, sales, prospecting, units sold, whatever the goal is for your company.

Time If you had homework due in school and it never had an end date, would you actually do it? Your goals are something you actually want to do, instead of something you have to do. But it still needs to be time-bound. So pick a date. Determine a reasonable time frame, and stick to it.

How long is this long-term goal? Is it five years out? Is ten years closer to your vision? Or maybe it's only two or three? Pick a specific date when this goal will be completed by.

Action Item

Create Your COVENANT Worksheet

Committed

You need to be dedicated to this goal. A goal is more than a wish or a hope—it's a pledge to yourself.

So how committed are you to your goal?

Let's say you were to work extremely hard for three months straight and don't really see any progress. Or maybe you see a bit of progress but it isn't like you hoped it would be. You are disheartened. Friends and family are telling you to give it up and move on.

Will you give up? Why?

_____

_____

_____

_____

Organized

Being organized is a recurring theme with millionaires reaching their goals. This means every employee knows what the goals of the company are and knows what systems need to be created to get there. To be truly organized you need to create systems so you aren't doing work twice. This step will be covered more in the next module.

Vision/Values

The goal needs to fit the rest of your life and the vision of your future. If your number-one priority is your family but your goal requires you to work 80 hours per week, the goal does not align with your vision or values.

Refer back to the True Values Worksheet (if complete) and Visioning Worksheet.

Does this goal align with your top four values?   YES   NO

If no, how can you make the goal align with those values?

_____

_____

_____

If you had the choice of achieving your goal but you had to compromise one or more of your values, would you do it?   YES   NO
Does this goal bring you one step closer to your complete vision? YES   NO

Enlightened

Being selfish with your goals is okay, but if you want to take your goals to the next level, you can not only have what you want but also help others in the process. That's when your goal becomes enlightened. It's helping others while you help yourself. Just like Zig Ziglar said:

"You can have everything you want in life, if you help enough other people get what they want."

Most eventual millionaires want to be financially free so they can help others. You can do that even before you become a millionaire, so let's incorporate it into your goal NOW.

How can this goal help others in the process?

_____

_____

_____

For example: You want to hit your revenue goal because you plan on giving 10% back.

Or you want to hire two key employees, not only to help your business, but also to provide them an amazing place to work with stability and flexibility for them and their family.

It then becomes a win-win situation.

Noticeable

Your goal needs to be seen. Once it's complete print it out and put it where you will notice it every single day. (A chart in your office, the whiteboard, on your desk, or make a plaque!)

Accountable

Use your mastermind group to keep you accountable to your goal. Tell them your goal and get their feedback about it. Then ask them to keep you accountable to that main goal EVERY week.

Numerical

Create a KPI (Key Performance Indicator). This is a number that will track your progress.

It should be something that you can measure now, view weekly to see your progress and it's how you know you have achieved your goal. It can be revenue, conversion rates, sales, prospecting, units sold etc.
What number do you want to use to track your goal?_____

Time-bound
Pick a date. Determine a reasonable time frame and stick to it.
When will this goal be completed?_____

Setting Short-Term Goals

You need to have that vision and you need to know what it is and keep it in plain view, but once you create a goal based on that, you break it down into smaller and smaller time frames. Then you only concentrate on the smallest and shortest goal in front of you.

Todd Tresidder said:

> You only want to work off what you can actually achieve within a confined time frame, otherwise you drop into overwhelm.

And you do. If you are an eventual millionaire, you have probably set goals before, big awesome goals. But what happens? You realize how huge they are and how long they are and how many years they will take you, and sometimes it can be discouraging.

The reason why you want to break it down to small steps is so that you only have to think about the next few days. You know exactly what you're doing the next few days and that's it. That way, you don't drop into overwhelm.

Brig Hart, a network marketer and founder of R3 Global, spoke about how many types of goals there are. He said:

> You know there are long-term, which, to me are 2 to 5 years but to most people it's 10 to 20. So to have long-term and then medium-range goals, which I equate to about a year or two, and then short-term goals, which are six months.

Then he breaks it down even further to mini-goals, which are 30- to 60-day goals, or 30- to 90-day, if that's easier for you. Then, from there, you have micro-goals and these can be anything from weekly goals to even 24-hour goals.

> Interestingly enough, it's easy to set a goal like "I want to be financially free in 10 years or so," but it's about the daily discipline that

we must do in order to hit our goal. You have to do your micro-goals before you hit your mini-goals. Micro-, then mini-, then short-, medium-, and long-term and if you don't do the daily things you're certainly not going to hit your short-term goals.

So set these goals, write them down, and then review them each day because if you can't measure your progress, you don't know whether or not you're making progress or maybe there is no progress at all. You have to have measurable goals in order to know if you're progressing.

How to Break Down the Goal

Many of my entrepreneurial clients have so many ideas on what they could be doing and what might bring in revenue that they can't figure out where to start. The solution? Work backward. Break it down! Break your Big Goal into three-, six-, and nine-month goals so you know where you need to be to reach your goal at each point in the year.

For example, let's say you want to earn $8,000 per month by the end of the year. Right now you earn $4,000 per month. Within six months you need to earn $2,000 more per month. And within three months you need to earn $1,000 more per month.

To make the goal of an extra $1,000 per month by March 31, you need to make $250 more per week.

Translate into products or services. Let's say you are a graphic designer. If you average about $250 per client, you need one more client each and every week.

So you set the objective "Get one additional client each week." That's a bit intangible. How do you get one more client per week? You may be thinking, "If I knew that, I would be making more already!"

The key is to know your numbers. If you are keeping track of your metrics already, you should know your closing rate—how many prospects you need to talk to in order to sell one person. If you don't know, start keeping track.

Let's say your closing rate is 50 percent. That means you only need to speak with two qualified prospects to gain one new client. But how many people do you need to talk to if you want to find two qualified prospects? If you don't already know at this point, look at your history of sales and make an educated guess.

Let's say you average one quality prospect for every six people you speak to. That means you need to have 12 conversations each week.

To meet your goal, brainstorm a list to accomplish just that one objective. Ask yourself: "How can I have 12 conversations each week?"

If you have conversations by networking events, how many do you need to go to? If you have conversations via e-mail, how many more visitors or subscribers do you need to attract to your website?

Fill out what your new goals are each quarter and write down the tasks you will need to do to accomplish them.

> **Date: Three-Month Goals—Earn $5,000 per Month by March 31.**
>> Get one additional client each week.
>> Have 12 conversations per week.
>> Go to two more networking events per month.
>> Create four guest posts to bring in traffic to the website.
>> Set up a system to keep in touch with qualified prospects.
>
> **Date: Six-Month Goals—Earn $6,000 per Month by June 30.**
> **Date: Nine-Month Goals—Earn $7,000 per Month by September 30.**
> **Date: One-Year Goals—Earn $8,000 per Month by December 31.**

Right now, commit to just the first three months. Decide that you will achieve your three-month goal come hell or high water. Declare that you will still be pursuing this goal in three months.

The *New York Times* shows that more than 80 percent of New Year's goals have failed by Valentine's Day. Commit to the goal for three months and afterward you can decide if that goal is right for your business. If not, modify it—but stick with it long enough to decide.

Now that you have objectives, how will you achieve them?

You are never going to know exactly what you are going to do every single step of the way. At the pace small businesses change, there is no way to predict what information you will need to know nine months from now.

You can, however, set up a system to figure out what to do next.

Once you start to break down the goal and realize what you need by when, then you can start to create your action plan.

Creating Your Action Plan

Your action plan is where you take that written goal and break it up into micro-goals, things with 30-, 60-, or 90-day timelines. We cannot predict every step, but we can look short term and figure out the best steps to start to take. Then we reevaluate the action plan once we have better and more accurate information. This melds the goal and the to-do list. This essential step I think is often missed.

Tony Hartl of Planet Tan said:

Don't focus on the big problem; focus on just the next step, because it's sort of like eating an elephant—just one bite at a time. Don't get overwhelmed by the entire goal, just look at the very next step, because success is a series of steps. It's not one big concept or one big great idea, at least not in my world, and it hasn't been one great idea, it has been a series to-dos and intense focus.

That's the point of an action plan. I work with many business owners who seem to reinvent the wheel for every piece of their business over and over again and that is not necessary. Trying to figure out a system or a routine that you do so you don't have to create every single day. We re-create and we re-create and we re-create what works and what doesn't work. That's why we test and we figure out what works and then we keep that. We don't have to keep making these decisions over and over and over again. So, in the worksheet we'll talk about this a little bit more. But in general, we want to think about the goal. What is that key point in your goal and how can we put that into our routine? I know your to-do list will change but your routine shouldn't. I've had clients of mine decide that Wednesdays are their marketing day and everything else is put on the back burner because marketing is so important in their business.

Figuring out those key actions that make up your routine is really important to keep continuous forward motion. Knowing every how or little to-do doesn't matter. It's a matter of having an idea of what those next steps might be and moving toward it.

Derek Sivers, who sold his company CD Baby for $22 million, said:

> You never know how plans are actually going to work. My plan completely changed only two weeks after launching and I think life is like that. It's like you can have some plans but once your plan hits the real world, the real world tells you what it wants to do and it's often not what you had planned. Anything I could say about my new venture now might just be moot in a few weeks.

You don't need to know the best strategy, the best tactic, the best tool until you're ready to use them. That also means that the action plan is very fluid. It can change based on your priorities and what the next best step will be.

So that's what we want to do when creating our action plan. What we'll do is write it for three months, but we're really making the next two or so weeks in actual detail and carving out a larger picture for what those three months look like.

We definitely need our mini- and micro-goals to help us know what we're going to concentrate on each week, but you don't really know your schedule more than two weeks at a time. The next two weeks you're going to be a different person. You are going to know different things than you know now.

Action plans prevent procrastination and the wrong actions. When you sit at your desk on Monday morning, does it take you a little while to figure out what the best thing to do is? If you finish up a task a little bit early, do you know what you need to do next or do you hop on social media or use that time in ways that won't help you hit that immediate goal? We need to know what the next actions to take are or we'll procrastinate or take the wrong ones.

Vonda White said:

> When you have your action steps and you start putting that into action towards it, you keep chipping away little by little at that goal, a little piece each week. You pretty soon have accomplished the goal and when you look back, let's say 12 months from now, you look back at that goal you've set for yourself. It might have seemed impossible or insurmountable in order to get to that point. But when you start doing it on a daily basis, a little bit at a time, it's kind of like that saying inch by inch, anything is a cinch. I really believe that because when I started my own company in 1996, I'd never owned my own company before.

Here are some questions to ask when creating your action plan:

What is the next best step?
Who can help me with this?
What information do I need right now?
What am I lacking today?
What can keep me from accomplishing my vision?

Keep moving forward. Keep moving forward. Keep moving forward. Do you notice a pattern? Keep moving forward. Most people know they need plans, but who actually does them? It's just like goals. It's hard to stick with a plan that's ever changing. We have too much on our plates anyway in general, let alone time to update a plan.

What I want you to come away with is this: it's not about having long to-do lists. It's not about the to-do list at all. It's a week-by-week plan of action. You want to know the biggest thing to do this week is to make sure you hit that goal. You want to know before you start your day what the most immediate actions are to take because this present moment is the only thing you have to make your goals a reality.

> Be consciously conscious of what you're focusing on. You're constantly conscious of your actions and looking at what results you're getting at all times and then shifting based on those results. It's conscious focused action. It's the key to doing anything you want and it's the key to making money.
>
> A lot of people want to start in the middle. They just want to go take massive action. Are you conscious of other things that have worked? Have you looked at information about what's the best way to do something? Have you looked at what your options are for your strategies? If you don't do all those pieces up front, you could be just completely wasting your energy taking the wrong actions. But a lot of people jump in at that level and it's just a huge mistake.
>
> —JV CRUM III

Action Feedback Knowledge Loop

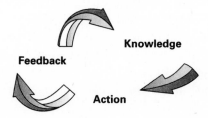

You need knowledge to make the right decisions on what action to take. But that's it. You don't need information overload. We use that as an excuse to procrastinate. Our brains will tell us we need more information before we can take that next step.

It's a really good excuse isn't it? Well, I need to know more information before I can start, before I can move forward, before I can spend my money. I need to know all the information humanly possible in order to take some action.

But most of the time it's just fear.

It doesn't matter if the knowledge stays in our head. We want it to come out and actually be used so we can reach the goals that we have for ourselves. You need some knowledge to make the right decisions on what actions to take. Only *some* knowledge. Because our society now has the Internet, we have tons of information at the tips of our fingers. That means instead of chatting with a friend and learning the next best action to take, we have to sift through hundreds of the best actions and decide on one. That's time consuming and frustrating.

I want to help you alleviate that. Right now decide to only learn for three reasons: to answer an immediate question, to research the next step, or for entertainment. I'm not saying you have to do this forever. Most of us *love* to learn. It's a passion. It helps us be well-rounded, amazing individuals. But there is only so much time in the week. So right now, while you are reading this book, pay attention to why you are getting your information.

So once you have some information on the next step, then you take the action. You might like it. You might hate it. You might feel dumb. You might be on top of the world. It might be some wonderful thing that happens. Whatever you feel, it's okay. Even if you hate it and say you never want to do it again. Just accept it and make note of it because then you get feedback from it. It will either work or not work. It'll give you details or insights that you can apply in other places and feedback is that quintessential amazing stuff that we really need in order to make our decisions.

Then you decide what you are going to do differently, how you can get a better result, and what improvements you can make for the next action. Then you decide what knowledge you need to fill in those gaps where you were previously lacking. That's why you don't need all of the information up front. You try and do small actions. Fail small. Do small actions so that way you just need the little pieces as you go. It's all about accomplishing things in small doses, gaining that feedback so you can incrementally get bigger and bigger. That's how you mitigate your risk.

And it might get messy. And that's okay! It will never be this clean, perfect world where you can learn and analyze and readjust perfectly.

Do what you can, when you can.

Matthew Tuttle of Tuttle Wealth Management said:

> We're constantly looking at what we're doing, ripping it apart, seeing if there is a better way to do it. Constantly looking at what's out there in the industry to see, number one, what everybody else is doing to again make sure we're staying different and number two, if there is anyone else out there who is doing something that really, really does seem good and we'll copy it and try to make it better.
>
> Some of our best ideas have come from things other people are doing that I'll look at and say, "All right, I like what they're doing there, how can I take it and how can I make it even better than what they're doing?" So we do a lot of that and we'll continue to do that for as long as we're around.

Action Item

Download the Action Plan Worksheet from http://EventualMillionaire.com/StarterKit to help you create your action plan.

Using a Mastermind Group for Accountability

As in Chapter 5, having a mastermind group, or someone to keep you accountable to these goals is critical. So if you haven't already, figure out what you will be doing to help you stay accountable to your goals and action plan.

Nolan Watson of Sandstorm Gold and Sandstorm Metals told me about what he does with a group of friends and business owners:

> We actually sit down once every three months and we write down our goals, everything from one month to three months to one year to five years and we hold each other accountable by saying things like hey you wrote that down three months ago. It has been three months and you still haven't done it.
>
> What's going on? Or they'll say, you just wrote down a five-year goal and that's way too easy. You should be able to accomplish that in the next 18 months or at least make a harder goal. So I find that writing down and knowing at the end of the

day that someone is going to call you on it if you don't do it is extremely beneficial.

It makes you do things not only to think about what you're trying to do and therefore guide some of your actions but it also makes you know that someone is going to call you on it if you don't do it. So eventually, you end up doing it.

This is a key factor that your mastermind group is going to help you with. Setting goals is extremely important but taking action to achieve those goals is even more important.

A lot of the millionaires talk about accountability and how important it is and that's why you have your mastermind group—to keep you there, to push you harder, and to make sure you're doing what you know you want to do.

If you have weekly mastermind sessions go over the wins that happen each week and write down what items you need to accomplish that week. Knowing what you need to do before the week begins is critical in making the right decisions ahead of time, and not only doing what is urgent and not important.

Achieving Goals

Take a look at your actions. You need to consciously bring attention to your goals each week.

Keep your actions and goals in an easily visible place. Some people keep them written in their bathrooms, while others choose to put them in their to-do lists, or next to their computers each week.

Set weekly priorities. Begin each week by determining what three things are most important to accomplish in your business. This means you will accomplish them even if you have to work late into the night. (Use your mastermind group for this, more about how at the end of the chapter.)

Figure out your priorities by setting aside time to plan your week. Your week should not only be about putting out fires. Your tasks each week should be bringing you closer to your goals.

Find a mastermind group, coach, or another business owner who can hold you accountable. You can create a great business without a good support network, but why would you want to? There will be tough days this year—days when you throw your hands up and say, "I'm frustrated! This isn't working!" Set up a support structure that can talk you off that ledge. Your accountability partners/ groups can also help by giving you their experiences and expertise.

You need to know what you want in order to go after it. Have fun figuring out what you want to go after in life! If you have listened to any of the interviews, you know that the possibilities truly are endless. We are only here on this earth for a short time. You want it to count. You want to be able to experience the things you want, to have the freedom and ability to see what life truly has to offer. And if you have children you want them to see the possibilities through you! You have so much power. Stop giving it to others and take it for yourself. It's not selfish. In fact, it's necessary.

We need more people who have goals and dreams for our future. We need people leading the way, to help others do the same. You are an Eventual Millionaire. Take time today for yourself and figure out what those dreams are. You can not only change your life with your goals, but many others, too!

ACTION ITEM REVIEW

Action Item

Create Your Vision

Step 1: The Future of Your Creating a Vision Is Experiencing What Your Life Will Be Like Long Term—Think about Yourself 10 Years or Even 20 Years in the Future

Who are you in your vision? Are you confident and conquering the world? Is that how you act now? Write a list of 10 characteristics that describe you in the future.

1. _____   6. _____
2. _____   7. _____
3. _____   8. _____
4. _____   9. _____
5. _____   10. _____

If you are having a hard time with this, find someone who you respect now and embodies the characteristics you want and write those down.

You can use these characteristics to grow. Daily work on each of these characteristics will move you forward fast. You can make amazing changes in a year to become the person that runs the company and the life you want.

Step 2: The Future of Your Business—Think about Your Business Long Term

- Where is the industry going? Will you be on the cutting edge?
- What has your business done in the past 10 or 20 years that has made it remarkable?

This will help you be ahead of the curve in your business, and we also work with these in the next module.

Step 3: Sum It Up!

Think about your life in 10 years. What do you want your life personally and professionally to look like?

Action Item

Do the exercises and create your crystal-clear vision. Then create your crystal-clear vision in just a few sentences. Write it down and create your goals based on it.

Action Item

Create Your COVENANT Worksheet

Commitment
Organized
Values/Vision
Enlightened
Noticeable
Accountability
Numerical
Time

Action Item

Download the Action Plan Worksheet from http://EventualMillionaire.com to help you create your action plan.

CHAPTER 8

Continuous Forward Motion

Just keep swimming!

—Dory, *Finding Nemo*

There really is no finishing in life, is there?

You're finished when you're dead. Until that day, there is always more to do, more to enjoy, more to *be*. It's the journey that counts, but remember that this is a never-ending journey. Even as you find success, there is always more.

What I've learned foremost with the successful people I've interviewed is that even as they hit their targets, even as they achieve their goals, another new shiny goal will come in its place.

That is both a wonderful and a terrible thing. It's wonderful because the amount of change, creation, and progress that one person can make is amazing. But the entrepreneurial mind is almost never satisfied with enough. It strives to do more and be more. It can feel like you are never doing enough or never living up to your potential.

It's that act of continuously striving and making incremental progress that counts. There are no overnight successes. It takes years. It's a series of small wins.

We can't guarantee the results. We can figure out the best actions to take to achieve those results and then do them. If they don't result in what we want, we have the opportunity to try again.

That is how you achieve success.

It seems we all want this amazing event to come hit us and blast us with a million dollars like the lottery. We want a big-business buyout, that amazing contact with someone who will make all of our dreams come true. So let's instead stop wishing for that.

Instead, let's start doing what millionaires do.

Millionaires in Forward Motion

MJ DeMarco, who became a millionaire with his online business, says that the path to a million is a process, not an event. It's a series of small steps. Brig Hart, a man who just hit the milestone of $300 million for his net worth, sums it up with this, "I discipline myself to do those things that cause progressive growth every day mentally, physically, and financially. I'd work out every day. I'd read a little bit every day. I'd encourage myself every day. I made contacts. I did my little bit every day." He says, "Input equals output."

Frank McKinney creates $30 million dream homes. He calls it the *lunch pail approach*. It's going to work every day and packing that lunch. It's those small things that matter and it takes work to do what you want in life.

We wish and hope it's this one event, one big break that brings success. It's meeting the right person, landing in a national magazine, or one amazing partnership. But really that's not the case at all. There is no such thing as an overnight success.

We hear these amazing success stories. Even on my web show, you'll listen to these amazing rags-to-riches stories. Yet we were not there, every single day, for the ups and the downs. A simple retelling of the story can never capture what it really took. It can't show you how they felt when they wanted to quit, or how hard it is to have a big deal fall through. They don't tell you about all of those days of so much work that felt really unproductive, or the constant questioning of whether this was the right step, or confusion about too many things and not enough time to successfully do them. An interview makes the continuous forward motion seem easy. It's not.

It's really easy to hear a success story from someone else. When you are trying to live through a success story, it's very different.

Continuous forward motion seems so intangible. Everyone is constantly moving! How do we know what will move us forward or not move us forward? How do we know if we are going in the right direction? You don't know. You can set goals, and failure can happen anyway. Right?

It's all a process, and we don't know the end of the story. All we can do is put in the work now that we think is the next best step.

Keep taking massive action in the direction you think is the right way. In looking at all of the interviews, each person just made the best decision they could with the information they had. That's all you can do. Make the best decisions you can with the information you have.

Focus, Patience, and Routine

So how do you create continuous forward motion? Three things: focus, patience, and routine. These are the what, why, and how for moving forward consistently.

Focus = What

Focus is something all too uncommon in business. Choosing what to make continuous forward motion on is critical.

Patience = Why

You will look at your peers making forward motion and think that you are not going fast enough. This is not a sprint. This is slow forward progress, and patience is a key skill to cultivate on this journey.

Routine = How

You cannot move forward without *moving*. Consistent action over the pieces that matter is how to make progress. Making those most important pieces part of your routine is how you do it.

These next sections give you tips and advice for keeping the ball rolling.

The Power of Focus

I've learned the hard way that when I was involved in many different things that I got a little bit done of a lot, and I couldn't figure out why I wasn't finishing things. It became incredibly obvious to me that I just was diluting myself. It was like I was just spinning plates and getting nowhere. For all of you listening that are like that and/or have experienced that, please embrace the value of extreme focus.

—LEN SCHWARTZ, PRO2PRONETWORK

Doing too many things at once will just water down what you are trying to achieve. The great management thinker and author Peter Drucker once said, "Don't tell me what you're doing, tell me what you've *stopped* doing." Most entrepreneurs like to say they have ADD, but the successful ones are able to harness that trait and use it to their advantage. That doesn't mean you can't get distracted. It *does* mean that you make a constant effort to focus in your business and personal lives.

Does this sound like you?

> As an entrepreneur my mind and probably like most entrepreneurs' minds are constantly open. We're constantly looking. A little bit of this is ADD I think. Sometimes I'm like squirrel at a laser light show.
> —Bobby Casey, Owner, Global Wealth Protection

> I am a pretty ADD kind of disorganized guy. I can't tell you the number of times I have written lists and plans and projections and then lost them and had to redo them. It's sort of like "ah man!"
> —David Hirschkop, Owner, Dave's Gourmet

Aaron Pitman said in the interview that he felt like he had ADD, but he went on to say:

> Eventually I learned that I can't tackle so many things at once and I need to laser focus and target focus. When I started to focus on certain tasks like just focusing on one business idea, things started to improve.
> —Aaron Pittman, Serial Entrepreneur

The more you focus, the more you'll act like a laser beam rather than a flashlight. You can burn through plastic with a laser. How powerful is that flashlight of yours?

Over and over and over the word *focus* comes up. It is a lesson that many of the people I interviewed have learned. Many have learned it the hard way. As you read this, you may already logically know these concepts. There is a *huge* difference between knowing these concepts and practicing these concepts.

Michael Port, best-selling author of *Book Yourself Solid*, is an amazing coach and speaker and works with many entrepreneurs. In our interview he summed up the difference between new entrepreneurs and successful ones.

Michael said:

> Newer entrepreneurs do this: Every time they get into something that's a challenge, they push everything that existed before and throw it away. They do a little bit of this, then a little bit of that. They're always flatlined because they're getting a little bit down the path with that one thing and then hit a big stumbling block so you say that's not the right path and start again.

Michael went on to say that successful entrepreneurs take one thing and focus on that one thing. They see a stumbling block and they do whatever it takes to break down that barrier and move on.

Focus: We All Have the Same Amount of Time

> Time is a created thing. To say "I don't have time" is like saying "I don't want to."
>
> —LAO-TZU

Just for a moment, clear everything off your agenda tomorrow. I mean everything. No work, no exercise, no eating, no watching the kids, no driving, nothing.

Your day is now completely free. Now imagine not adding any to-do items in the whole day. Nothing to do. No TV and no Facebook or Twitter. No phone. No sleeping. No going for a walk. Just sitting and being.

How long would tomorrow feel?

Those 24 hours would pass very slowly.

You only have so much time. But what you do in that time makes up you and your life. Are you choosing the things you want? Take responsibility that you got yourself where you are right now. This is a result of your decisions. Your time is completely full because of you.

How Many Priorities Can You Juggle?

> The one thing that I've gotten smarter in my old age is that I focus. I'm big on not biting off more than I can chew. So it seems like I have a lot of things going on, I'm very focused. You can juggle five balls but if you try and juggle six, all six fall

down. I think that you need to be very smart today and you'll learn this with wisdom as you get older and having a couple of companies fail on you.

—CHRIS GRAVAGNA, SERIAL ENTREPRENEUR AND
FOUNDER OF WINESBYWIVES.COM

One key piece of focusing is knowing how much you can actually concentrate on. So where is your max capacity? As human beings, we cannot hone in on just one thing at a time, as we are constantly forced to make decisions quickly. Do I need food or shelter more? And so on. Like life, a business needs more than one piece for it to work. First, you need to know what you are capable of achieving. Each person is unique. It depends on your traits, and how efficient you are with certain tasks and subjects. If you feel like things are falling apart right now, look at what you are doing. You are probably past your max capacity.

Action Item

Create a simple list of all of the business pieces you are taking care of. Use the list below to help.

Aspects of Your Business

Sales
Marketing
Accounting
Managing
Administration
Customer Service
Custodial
Providing the Product or Service

Aspects of Your Personal Life

Cleaning
Maintenance of House
Feeding Yourself and Your Family
Hygiene
Taking Care of Your Children
Hobbies and Fun

Look at how many things you have going on! You should be proud of all of the things you can handle right now.

If things are falling apart, then the list you have right now is too much! If you have a good handle on things then you know how much you can handle.

> The one thing I would recommend, a lot of us, we create all of these different things we need to do but we never really finish anything. So just picking one to two or three things that you know you can accomplish this week, actually making it a priority and getting it done. Usually by focusing on the small stuff though it gets you much closer to the kind of results and the kind of success that you want to see.
> —SEAN MALARKEY, ONLINE MARKETER SEANMALARKEY.COM

Focus: Setting Clear Priorities   Do you not like the choices you are making?

Everything in life has a choice. I've heard others say, "Paying bills is not a choice!" but it is. We choose to pay our bills because we want the services more than the money. We choose to work because we want the income, and everything the income provides. If you don't like these choices you are free to change them, but they are hard choices to make.

Absolute Yes   I like to use the tool called the Absolute Yes. Whenever you are confronted with a choice, ask yourself, "Is this an absolute _yes_?"

This method helps you determine things that are in your schedule that you don't want to do but think you should. For example, when you receive an invitation to a graduation party, ask yourself "Is this an absolute _yes_?" Do you really want to go to this party, or do you think you _should_ go?

Even if your answer is a no, it doesn't mean you won't go. It is asking the question that helps. It makes you more aware of the events that you _want_ to participate in. You make a conscious choice that it is not an absolute yes, but you still want to go. Because of the conscious effort beforehand, you no longer think that you could have been doing something better.

When you're either new in business or you're hurting and you need money, you find yourself saying yes to a lot. When I started saying no because I could not dilute myself anymore, it felt strange. I got so used to saying yes, yes, yes, I didn't realize I was just spinning my wheels.

So just start saying no. If what's being offered to you doesn't fit what you're looking to accomplish in your life, the answer has to be no and you've got to be okay with that.

—LEN SCHWARTZ, OWNER PRO2PRO NETWORKING

One tip I have for the people pleasers who love to say yes (which I am, and many of my clients are, too!), if you can't say no right away, just say "Maybe." It allows you to go away and think about it before jumping in and saying yes. It also allows you to avoid making up an excuse on the spot because you want to say no but also be nice about it.

For every situation that isn't an absolute yes, you can always say maybe, go away, think about it for sure and then come back and let them know. That way you have a chance to decide what you actually want, not what is best for the person asking.

Should   We cloud our choices with the things we *should* be doing. I *should* volunteer because that's what a good person does. I *should* send a birthday card. I *should* exercise. Don't should on yourself.

When we use the word *should*, it devalues our choices. Sending a birthday card, because you always do, or because they sent you one first, is not a **conscious choice**. Sending out a birthday card without conscious intention drains your energy, because part of you doesn't want to be doing it.

If you only do what you *should* be doing instead of what you *want* to be doing, you will not like your choices. The reason? They are not your choices, they come from outside sources. The word *should* implies that someone else thinks the choice is right. Our to-do lists are full of *shoulds*.

The best way to combat choices that are not your own is to set your priorities. Once you determine what you *want* to do, and put them first, the things you *should* do lessen.

Deciding What to Choose If you ask yourself "Is this an absolute *yes?*" and you do not know the answer, then you need to take time to figure out what you do want.

In *Alice in Wonderland,* Alice needed to choose a path. She asked the Cheshire Cat which direction to choose. The cat asked where she was trying to go, but Alice replied, "Anywhere, as long as I go somewhere." The cat replied, "If you don't care where you're going, it doesn't make a difference which path you take."

If you do not know your priorities and what you would like to enjoy in life, then you end up with a life you do not enjoy. It's not a life that you control, it's a life that controls you.

A great resource to help you both personally and in business is a website called LessDoing.com.

The creator of the site, Ari Meisel, has an amazing story of being very sick and learning how to take care of that with nutrition, but he also has amazing tips and resources for taking control back over your time. *You* have a choice in your life.

Action Item

Choose your own *focus*. Because you have your one goal from Chapter 7, this should be a bit easier.
Choose *one* thing to focus on in business.
Choose *one* thing to focus on personally.

The Power of Patience

Patience is the capacity to accept or tolerate delay, trouble, or suffering without getting angry or upset.

Instant gratification seems to be a trend in the world today. We want everything on demand. I heard a joke from a comedian who said, "A friend was complaining about his GPS taking way too long. He was annoyed and kept saying, 'Why isn't this going faster?'"

The comedian chimed in, "Oh, I don't know, maybe because it has to go to *space!*"

We tend to want everything now even if we know there is supposed to be a longer process. In fact, that was one of the issues that

I had that landed me $70,000 in debt. I wanted to be successful and have everything my parents had. When I was 20 years old, I had a cute house and two cars. It didn't even occur to me that it had taken my parents many years of hard work before they were able to buy their first house.

Even now I am working on improving my patience. I chose spending more time with my children over the growth of my business. It's a choice that I know in my heart is right but it's a learning curve to be patient!

Learning Patience

Frank McKinney, who builds $30 million dream homes and runs ultramarathons through Death Valley, has this to say about starting out too fast:

> In ultramarathon, there is a saying: "Start slow and slow down." I've learned that from the best. There are some of these hot shots that will take off, the start gun goes off and by Mile 40 there's an ambulance coming by to pick them up off the side of the road because they just, yeah they're two hours ahead of me but you know what, they burned out. They flamed out. It's the same thing in business or a significant undertaking.

Have you noticed this in your own life or business? Have you sprinted out of the starting gate only to fizzle out shortly down the road?

There are many reasons why we fizzle out when we jump in too quickly. We are excited and looking for quick results. That energy wanes when the day-to-day tasks become mundane. And if you're putting a ton of energy in and not seeing many results, you'll wonder why even bother!

I think the answer in both of these cases has to do with patience. We have to have the patience to start slow and conserve our energy. We have to have patience to continue on a path that has obstacles and issues or when you might not be seeing a lot of results!

I see this often when people are starting businesses. They are excited and bubbling with ideas. They try one, and are extremely excited about it, and then it fizzles. They think that the idea will "take off," and when it doesn't they turn to the next idea. Then they try that, but that doesn't take right away either. Then they have a series of false starts. I know this because that was me when I first started as an entrepreneur. I had a provisional patent filed, an iPhone app, and blog all started within three months. Three separate things that had nothing to do with each other. I'm glad I saw them through to an end, and didn't just give up, but I do think that I was way too excited and impatient on waiting for things to "hit." There is no get rich quick. You can win the lottery, and that makes it more likely you will go bankrupt. The Certified Financial Planner Board of Standards estimates that nearly one-third of lottery winners will become bankrupt. Jumping into getting money without the process of learning how to use it and earn it seems to be a recipe for disaster.

It's that process that is necessary. And within that process are times when you want to give up. Achieving any worthwhile goal has obstacles.

So what do you do when you are faced with that fizzle? Or not seeing results? Or wanting to give up?

Frank McKinney's example:

> When we're confronted with those debilitating moments in life, using Bad Water as the metaphor and that Mile 92 situation as the metaphor, what do you do? Every cell in my body is screaming, 'It's fine for you to stop! You're not feeling well.' My wife is there trying to revive me. My crew is there. Or with faith, patience and the passage of time, might I revive? So I might remain flat on the ground for a half an hour until that debilitating moment or sensation passes.
>
> Then I have a choice. I can choose to pack everything up and go back to the hotel and pack up my suitcase, maybe probably go to sleep and then in the morning when I go to shave, how can I face myself in the mirror? You quit. Or, maybe I'm still feeling terrible, I put my running shoes back on, my sunglasses and my hat and I just start shuffling toward the finish line. Not running, not necessarily even walking, just dragging my feet toward the finish line. Relentless forward motion. It doesn't matter how fast I'm going as long as I am going in the right direction, faith paces you in the passage of time.

Patience in the passage of time. I will eventually recover. Now that was something I learned from that race and I use that in my daily life.

Patience and Balance in Your Journey

What happens when you have everything in your life competing for your attention? We can use the power of focus in many aspects. But what if you love your business and love your family? That is something that many entrepreneurs, especially entrepreneurial moms, deal with often. How can we achieve balance, and is balance a myth?

Marissa Levin, who built a great company called Information Experts, said:

> One of the things that I tell people is that I have had to sacrifice the growth of my company for the development of my children and that's okay and I would make those choices again in a heartbeat. You have to just really be gentle and kind with yourself and do all that you can do and not compare yourself to others and not get frustrated if things aren't moving as fast as you want them to move with the business. Just trust the process and continue to try to enjoy the journey and stay focused on why you're doing what you're doing. I would definitely say that time management, I mean that's kind of the biggest struggle I see is that people just don't know where to put the limited number of hours. They're pulled in a lot of places. It's just there's a lot of competing demands for people's time.

I'm not sure we will ever solve the work/life balance, because it's different for everyone, but I can say that both in my life and the lives of the people I've interviewed I have found that having patience with yourself and the situation makes a huge difference. Accepting or at the least tolerating the delay or trouble that comes up in your life will serve you and everyone around you.

We have so many demands on us. Even when we thought technology would improve our efficiency (which it has in many cases) there are always things to step in right behind it. That's the world we live in now. It's up to you to take control and only say yes to the things that are most important to you.

The Power of Your Millionaire Routine

Right now, start thinking about what millionaire habits you add to your routine every day. What are those things that are going to be bringing you closer to your goals? How many hours do you plan on working on your business every single week? How many hours are you going to take to read this book and do the actions? The work takes work! You have to go ahead and sit your butt in the chair and do the work to get the results. So what are those habits that are going to take you there?

I want you to think about what your possible millionaire routine would be. A routine is just a sequence of actions, like a fixed program, but I want you to start writing this down ahead of time, knowing what you're going to be doing that next day, starting to plan that sort of thing so that way the continuous forward motion makes sense. Just like Frank McKinney's lunch pail approach. It's those small things that add up to a massive amount What is that routine that you are doing every single day that's going to take you forward?

You may think you aren't the routine type. I have heard more than the excuse "I just can't do a routine. I'm not that kind of person." I understand that! A lot of creative people thrive on change and settling into a routine seems impossible.

But usually I ask this question, "Do you brush your teeth every morning?" The answer is always yes. Then I ask, "Do you eat breakfast?" Most of the time it's yes. That's a routine. It doesn't have to happen at the same time every day. But it does happen every day.

Taking Care of Yourself

Brig Hart, a man who just hit the milestone net worth of $300 million, sums it up with this:

> I disciplined myself to do those things that caused progressive growth every day, mentally, physically, financially. I'd work out every day. I'd read a little bit every day. Encourage myself every day. Made contacts. Do my little bit every day. Because input equals output.

Now here is where the line between personal and professional gets fuzzy. When you are an entrepreneur it is very difficult to separate the two. It can be both a blessing and a curse! On the days when you are mentally or physically not feeling great your business will suffer. So we need to pay attention and be in peak condition to further our goals every day. That means paying attention to our mental and physical state every single day.

I noticed something with the millionaires that I interviewed. Out of more than 100 who I interviewed, only a small handful are overweight. That was an amazing fact to me, because if you look at the statistics of the United States:

> CDC.gov says the percentage of adults over the age of 20 who are overweight or obese is 69.2 percent (2009 to 2010).

So if these successful people I interviewed were typical, 69 of them would be overweight. That's not the case. They take care of themselves.

In the book *The 4-Hour Work Week* by Tim Ferriss, billionaire entrepreneur Richard Branson was asked how to become more productive:

> He leaned back and thought for a moment. The tropical sounds of his private oasis Necker Island murmured in the background. Twenty people sat around him at rapt attention wondering what the billionaire's answer would be to one of the big questions, perhaps the biggest question of business. Then he broke the silence. "Work out."
>
> He was serious and elaborated. Working out gave him at least four additional hours of productive time per day. The cool breeze punctuated his answer like an exclamation point.

Who wouldn't like *four* additional hours of productive time per day?

Frank McKinney elaborates on how creating a healthy body makes a huge difference in your success:

> I run six miles every other day and some of the greatest ideas and concepts come to me when my mind is free. So exercise provides quiet time in which to come up with some great ideas and new concepts. Chemical changes that take place in the mind and the body, which are very conducive to allowing you to come up with those creative concepts and, as a byproduct,

I haven't even gotten into this part, but you're healthier. So it goes without saying, most people exercise to be healthy but *businesspeople exercise for an advantage.*

Businesspeople exercise for an advantage. Did you ever imagine that? What are you doing to move your body? Do you feel better when you exercise?

This is not a diet book, but I truly think there is a link between success and taking good care of yourself. It's especially hard to live healthy when you have huge goals and so much to do already. Eating right can be put on the back burner.

When I asked the millionaires about their diets, Brenton Hayden, who built a business to help owners lease their properties, said, "I wish. The entrepreneur's diet is late night large meals after skipping all meals through the day."

I dug a little deeper and asked in a survey if there is a certain way millionaires take care of themselves and eat. Or is there any theme to pay attention to?

The majority (55 percent) of the millionaires surveyed had a clean diet. Their specific eating habits varied, among them no gluten, no sugar, and a diet high in fruits and vegetables. Many paid attention to organics and didn't eat fried foods.

The others didn't pay much attention to diet. They ate when they were hungry and when they had time. It's interesting that many eventual millionaires strive to be better and make progress in many areas of business but may neglect nutrition But cognitive function can be greatly enhanced by eating the right foods.

I interviewed Dr. John Berardi, millionaire and owner of Precision Nutrition. He had this advice for entrepreneurs:

> The first thing I think is that fitness and nutrition needs to be defined as a priority in your life. What most of us do when it comes to fitness, in particular entrepreneurs who like projects, is we make fitness a project.
>
> I'm going to solve fitness now, and then I'll get to my other projects again. When has life ever worked that way? The only way to do this is full integration. It's to find the things that you can do and sustain. Find one thing that you can do today for the next two weeks to sustain and then add another one after.

That's the only way human beings change, and it's the only way human beings can sustain effort in the long run.

We start our clients on a basic exercise practice routine. We have them practice exercises. It doesn't take very long. You don't even need to go to the gym. You just devote 10 or 15 minutes to this exercise practice. You can just get up from your desk. Then what we do is we start them off on a fish oil supplement, multivitamin, and a probiotic supplement.

One thing very few people realize is that there's this constant dialogue between your gut and your brain. Some people have called the stomach a second brain because it produces a lot of the same hormones and neurotransmitters your brain does. If your gut bacteria is out of alignment, things like cognitive test scores go down. Depression goes up. Fish oil, a multivitamin and probiotic supplement, help with that connection.

There were two cool studies I ran across a few years ago. One was in prison inmates, and what they did was they just gave them a fish oil capsule and a multivitamin each day. Then they looked at cognitive performance, violence, antisocial behavior, all the things that you want to be better in prison. There was like a 60 percent reduction in violence and antisocial behavior from just doing that. So the question is what's magical about a multivitamin and fish oil? Nothing. What's magical is not being deficient in stuff. When you're deficient, brains don't work right. Bodies don't work right. So what they thought was "I wonder if this would work with kids." They gave kids the same, fish oil and a multivitamin. ADHD symptoms way down. Cognitive test scores way up. Antisocial behavior, violence change for the better. It's just one of these things where for any entrepreneur who's like "How do I use nutrition to feel better tomorrow," step one get nutrition deficiencies removed. You've got to get rid of them.

Action Item

Take the smallest action that will have a meaningful outcome with your food and exercise, and start paying attention to that one thing. You have permission to ignore everything else.

Taking Care of Business

Over and over, millionaires reference the importance of reaching the top in your industry or business:

> To become a chess grandmaster also seems to take about 10 years. (Only the legendary Bobby Fischer got to that elite level in less than that amount of time: it took him nine years.) And what's 10 years? Well, it's roughly how long it takes to put in 10,000 hours of hard practice. Ten thousand hours is the magic number of greatness.
>
> —MALCOLM GLADWELL

To be a millionaire, which is the definitive goal that tops most people's wealth scales in the United States, you must start by setting goals right at the beginning. That means more than just setting goals for a specific net worth.

The best way to be at the top is to keep making continuous forward motion toward the top. That means creating a routine that will serve you. Create this routine in business, but also spiritually, mentally, and physically.

What are those things that you want to work on every day to hit greatness? If we are looking at *hours* of work on something, what do you want to be progressing? Think about your goal from Chapter 7. Imagine that you are chatting with a millionaire who has already achieved that goal. What did they do every day to get there? What was so consistent in their lives that it made it almost impossible for them not to reach that goal?

> I think that persistence is the most important attribute for an entrepreneur to have. Without, you're just not going to be able to succeed.
>
> —IAN IPPOLITO, vWORKER (FORMERLY KNOWN
> AS RENTACODER.COM)

Ian referenced research by researcher Angela Lee Duckworth, PhD, an assistant professor of psychology at the University of Pennsylvania. Angela studies non-IQ competencies that predict success both academically and professionally. Her research populations have included West Point cadets, National Spelling Bee finalists, novice teachers, salespeople, and students.

Her findings were not that the more talented people were more successful, nor was it a person's IQ. But there were a few characteristics she said determined high success. She sums them up into one word:

Grit.

Duckworth said:

> One of them was the tendency not to abandon task from mere changeability sake. Changing around a lot is not a way to get anywhere. Having perseverance in the face of adversity, setbacks, failures, that is important.
>
> Self-discipline, which is being able to resist temptation, is also an important quality, but not such an important quality when it comes to high achievement.
>
> In the National Spelling Bee competition, the students are studying anywhere from an hour a week to scarily 35 or 40 hours a week but what differentiates kids who are gritty from kids how are not gritty is not just the hours of work that they are putting in, but that they are putting the hardest kind of work in.
>
> They are not studying the words they are already know, they're not sitting around being quizzed on what's coming easily, they isolate what they don't know, they identify their own weaknesses and then they work just on that. And that seems to be characteristic of high achievement and what grit enables you to do.

Millionaire Routines

> A daily routine is just so key. When I first got serious about network marketing, my goal was to get 20 no's per day. I did that for 6 months, and the seventh month was a $40,000 month.
>
> —RAY HIGDON, RAYHIGDON.COM

Let's take a look at some of the everyday routines of some of the successful millionaires.

Hugh Culver is a motivational speaker on leadership. He says:

> We have these cycles of every 90 minutes throughout the day and so the first cycle starts as soon as you wake up. For every 90 minutes of the day you have this high and then you're followed

by a low. The things I would recommend to any entrepreneur, if you really want to become a millionaire, is you have to reexamine what you do with the first 90 minutes of your day. If you're the kind of person that works from home, then that would be the first 90 minutes in the morning.

For some of you, you need to get up earlier because what's happening is you're missing out on some of the best times of the day. So staying up late and watching Netflix or some DVD is probably not going to serve you as much as getting a little bit more sleep and getting up early in the morning and using that precious time. So the thing I would recommend is reexamine the first 90 minutes of your day. Now, if you make your income at the office, then I would absolutely recommend what you do for the first 90 minutes of the day in the office and so what you need to be looking at is how is it I can reduce the amount of interruptions and distractions?

How is it that I can get done what's on my agenda, the things that are important to me first? And how is it that I can create the highest level of achievement in those 90 minutes? Like what do I have to do, so I am thinking to myself "wow" like I got a big thing done—like I've got this big cross through the list of this blog posting, client proposal, reaching out to my network. draft e-mail, draft teleseminar line; like what did I get done that I could never have gotten done any other time of the day? That's what I would recommend.

Jeffrey J. Fox, CEO of Fox & Company consulting, said:

To becoming a millionaire. Number one, they should take a day or an hour or something and just work on their business instead of in their business. What is the difference? On their business is where they're plotting strategy and so forth and thinking what they're going to do next.

They're working on the business versus in the business, which is you're a dry cleaner and you're ironing pants and cleaning shirts and folding them and hanging them. That's working in the business. You know, paying the bills is working in the business.

I guarantee you all your listeners have on their calendar blocked out Thanksgiving and Christmas and Sundays, right? So why don't they do the same thing for their business?

Typical Day Examples

A glimpse into a millionaire's routine with Todd Tresidder:

I typically wake up early and without alarm—5:30ish during summer and 6 A.M. during winter. My wife and I alternate morning routines. Every other day I work out and she does the family morning routine by making breakfast and getting the kids off to school. The following day we switch roles, alternating back and forth. Workouts vary with the season. My staple is running.

From an exercise perspective, this gives a good rest day in between workouts, which is important for injury prevention while also providing the mental clarity and focus that regular exercise brings to our lives. I usually get two days of clear thinking and focus for every hard work out.

I learned this about myself back in college. I discovered that I got better grades when I studied less and played basketball every other day. I later added a running routine as well. The increased focus was more valuable than the lost study time. I've continued the pattern ever since.

Also, from a productivity perspective, this gets my workout done early in the morning leaving the entire day for focused, productive work. I used to exercise in the middle of the day (because I could), but I found it chewed up nearly half of every other day taking a huge chunk out of productivity.

Billy Murphy, BlueFire Poker and ForeverJobless.com

7 A.M. Breakfast
7:30 Workout
9:00 Protein shake
9:10 Shower
9:30 E-mails and work
10:00 Lunch
10:30 Drive to office
10:45 Work and prepare for calls
11:00 Calls or meetings
12:30 Lunch #2
1:00 Calls or meetings
3:00 Protein bar

3:10 E-mails and work

3:45 Read business blogs or articles

4:15 Work on writing content for ForeverJobless, or responding to readers' comments

4:45 Protein peanut butter balls

4:55 Try to complete any outstanding tasks that need to be done

5:45 Reviewing businesses for sale, or ideas that I'm looking into

6:15 E-mails and work

6:45 Review signups/traffic

7:00 Call w/business friends updating/strategizing about what we're working on

7:30 Try to organize a bit of a schedule for the next day

7:45 Drive home

8:00 Dinner

8:30 Meeting up with a friend or date

9:30 E-mails and work

10:00 Reading or watching entrepreneur interviews until sleep, or sometimes watching part of a movie

11:00 Sleep

Creating Your Millionaire Routine

Routines may be easy to start but the real challenge is to be able to continue doing them every day. How do people stay consistent? What has worked *best* for most successful millionaires? How do you make the decision every day to keep doing your morning routine?

It's important to take action toward your goals to achieve success.

Each millionaire calls it something different. I like to call it your *Millionaire Routine*.

What are the items that you need on your to-do list every day or each week that will achieve your dreams?

We all know plans and ideas will change over time. What are those things that will remain constant?

- Are you more productive when you exercise?
- Do you need to meet three prospects per day to hit your sales goals?
- Do you have to take one action each day to hit your target of website visitors?

Action Task

Detail what your millionaire routine looks like:

Millionaire Routine

1._____

2. _____

3. _____

4. _____

5. _____

I recommend including no more than five items on the list.
Then commit to this list. The day isn't complete until you finish this routine.

We tend to let things distract our routine such as e-mails and so on. Go ahead and get distracted but it will mean you will stay up late to get your routine items done!

Knowing what millionaires do doesn't matter. Doing what millionaires do does matter.

Continuous Forward Motion

This is all much easier said than done. But just like MJ DeMarco said, "It's a process." You don't need to implement every single system right away. You do need to keep this one idea in your head though: *Continuous Forward Motion*. If you are moving forward on a daily basis, adding up those small wins, then you are a success. And if you already know that you will do that, then you can relax a bit, you are already successful.

ACTION ITEM REVIEW

Action Item

Create a simple list of all of the business pieces you are taking care of. Use the list below to help.

Aspects of Your Business

Sales
Marketing
Accounting
Managing
Administration
Customer Service
Custodial
Providing the Product or Service

Aspects of Your Personal Life

Cleaning
Maintenance of House
Feeding Yourself and Your Family
Hygiene
Taking Care of Your Children
Hobbies and Fun

Action Item

Choose your own *focus*. Since you have your one goal from Chapter 7 this should be a bit easier.

Choose *one* thing to focus on in business.
Choose *one* thing to focus on personally.

Action Item

Take the smallest action that will have a meaningful outcome with your food and exercise, and start paying attention to that one thing. You have permission to ignore everything else.

Action Task

Detail what your millionaire routine looks like:

Millionaire Routine

1._____
2. _____
3. _____
4. _____
5. _____

I recommend including no more than five items on the list.

Then commit to this list. The day isn't complete until you finish this routine.

CHAPTER

Stories of Millionaires Before They Were Millionaires

I love a good rags-to-riches story, but I before I started talking to millionaires personally, it seemed like they were a different type of person than I. Like I said before, I thought that they must have had a special mind-set, or that they knew the right people, or that they were smarter than me. They made it look so easy. One day they were broke, and a year later they were rich! That is how it seemed.

Success stories are easy to tell when you just talk about the positive things. People usually skip over the hard parts, the waking up at 3 A.M. in a cold sweat because you don't know how you are going to afford your bills. Even now, when I ask millionaires about the failures and hard parts, the pain is subdued because of the passage of time. But those hard times, those doubts, those thoughts of "I'm not good enough" or "Can I really do this?" are all there.

One thing that I have learned after all of these interviews is that no matter what walk of life we are from, we are all just people, money or no money, success or no success. We are just people trying to make sense of the world and do our best. And if you have a desire to do more and better things with your life, all you need is that desire. Everything else you'll encounter is just a series of obstacles to overcome. Lacking money, time, or knowledge does not stop someone with the desire to improve his or her life and the lives of others.

Here are the stories from millionaires about before they were millionaires, before they knew they would be successful. I hope you see some of yourself in these stories, because I want you to see that you, too, can push the limits of your success and enjoy your life and business while you are earning your million.

Brad Deal

Before: Owned business in auto industry
Business: Sticks and Stones

> I would say if you don't have anything patentable you have got to do everything in your power to get yourself out there and get your brand built up as soon as you possibly can.
> —BRAD DEAL

Brad's three-year-old daughter came up with their business idea. In fact, it wasn't a business idea at all. "When my daughter was little, we loved walking along our riverfront with her. She'd get out of her stroller and run around. One time she just happened to point and say, 'A.' I looked over and saw a branch that looked like the letter and said, 'Yep, that's an A.' Then we kept walking a little bit farther, and she said, 'H.' She saw another shape that looked like a letter, and I agreed."

They started making it a game to find the letters in nature and architecture. Brad and his wife, Jera, wanted to teach their daughter how to read by using the letters they found outside, so they started taking photos of them. When her preschool teacher was going to get married, they wanted to give her a special gift. Brad and Jera decided to use the photos they had taken and create a keepsake by framing her teacher's new last name.

Brad said, "Within a day or two of giving that gift, we probably had three or four different people who wanted one. One person wanted seven or eight for Christmas gifts. At that point I realized that it could be hot, but I certainly wasn't thinking that this was going to be our career and our livelihood. I thought it might be some nice extra income."

The business started to grow by word of mouth. People would call them because they had seen one of the photo keepsakes at a neighbor's house. They started getting more and more people coming to their home to buy the artwork. There were always pho-tos of letters scattered on the kitchen table. Soon they realized they wouldn't be able to keep running the business from their house.

Brad had a friend who owned a Hallmark store, so they started taking orders there. But Brad knew he had to get online. The opportunities online would be a lot greater than in their home-town in Illinois alone. The online business started to grow, and they started to get mentioned in quite a few local newspapers. Since they were growing so quickly, they hired more people.

Brad knows the power of creating relationships. He used to love to go to the *Oprah* show when it was on. One time, before the show, he was singled out (he was one of the few men there!) by the woman who prepped the crowd to go on stage. Oprah wasn't there, but he ended up chatting with her in front of the whole audience. "At one point, she said, 'You took the day off work to bring your wife here. That was nice!' I said, 'Well, I own my own company, so it wasn't that hard to do.' Then she asked me, 'What's your company?' So it gave me a chance to promote.

"We sent a keepsake to the lady that got us the tickets as a thank-you. Within a couple of weeks, the woman that had called me up on stage called me and said, 'I'd love to get one for a bar mitz-vah that I'm going to,' and I said, 'No problem, I'll send you one!' So we had a few keepsakes rolling around at Harpo."

Brad and his wife really wanted to go on the *Oprah* show, and one day the show called them. They weren't initially invited to be on the show, but to be part of a special studio audience about mil-lionaire moms. "We quickly learned that a special audience was basi-cally like the regular audience. You just come in a different door."

"We brought a keepsake to give to Oprah, but security confis-cated it. When you first come in the studio, you have to show secu-rity your ID. My wife and I told them that we had brought this gift for Oprah, but they said, 'We're just being honest with you, you're not going to get to give that to her.' So we just left it with them fig-uring that if worse came to worst, somebody would get a nice keep-sake that says Oprah."

At the end of the show, Oprah was gracious enough to chat with the audience and take questions for almost an hour. "My wife is rib-bing me, saying, 'Stand up, raise your hand!' So I raised my hand. Oprah called on me, and I stood up and said, 'Hey, my wife and I made a gift for you. I appreciate you having us to your show. Would you be willing to accept it?' She said, 'Sure.' No sooner had she said that than the woman who originally called me up on stage during the last episode was standing there with our wrapped gift. Someone gives Oprah these giant gleaming scissors brought out to her. You only see these kinds of scissors in the movies—I mean, they're giant, and they're gleaming. Somebody was probably shining them before they came out!

"So they bring the scissors out, and she cuts the ribbon off delicately at the perfect angle, and she opens it right there in front of everybody. She really, genuinely, I think, liked it a lot. She started asking us all these questions about our present to the point where somebody behind me started muttering, 'I wish these guys would just sit down.'

"Every time I tried to sit down, she asked me to stand up again. She told her production studio to turn the cameras off for a minute. She said that she would love to give this as a gift to Tom and Katie for their wedding. 'Could you make one for me?' We, of course, said, 'Sure!'"

After that show, they received a lot more press. They were on *The Big Idea with Donny Deutsch,* then in Oprah's magazine and *People* magazine. But they still had to do a lot of work to get their press. They hired a public relations company that got them on the *Rachael Ray* show.

After years of work and marketing they have a very successful multimillion-dollar company. From having customers pick out photos on their kitchen table to an amazing website where you create it yourself, they have grown one step at a time.

Brad gives this advice, "Whatever the next thing on your to-do list is, do that now. Many ideas never got off the ground and got marketed, simply because somebody was either afraid to do it, or they were too lazy to do it. So I would say whatever the next thing on your to-do list is, go do it."

Briana Borten

Before: Worked at a spa
Business: The Dragon Tree Spa/Imbue Pain Patch

I knew that I would do anything I had to do. It's really important to me to do what I say I am going to do so when I took a loan from family I thought "If the business fails, what would I have to do in order to pay off those debts and where would I live?" I thought I can live in a tiny little apartment and I could eat Ramen noodles and work 10 jobs and I could pay them back. I had so much confidence in my own ability to do whatever I had to. I would work my whole life and I would be willing to live very frugally to make sure I paid back everything.

—BRIANA BORTEN

What started out as a way to relieve pain for her broken neck paved the way for the Dragon Tree Spa owner and Imbue pain patch manufacturer Briana Borten.

Briana was an exuberant teenager who dreamed of traveling and making it big in the art world. However, fate had a different plan for her. She was in art school when a tragic car accident left her with a broken neck similar to Christopher Reeve's injury. She was a hair's-breadth away from being paralyzed but thankfully, continuous therapy sessions left her in the pink of health once again. This prompted her to take a closer look at what she wanted to do with her life.

Briana was 20 years old when the thought of opening her own spa appealed to her, despite having zero knowledge and experience, not to mention funds, about opening a business. What she had, though, was sheer determination and the will to help others through the wonders of massage, herself being one of those who benefited greatly from it. Before she took on the challenge, she first traveled to Europe and the Czech Republic and even ran a hostel to satisfy her wanderlust. When she got back to Oregon, she decided to plunge head-on and enrolled herself in a massage school. There she received formal training and became a massage therapist.

While some would be too arrogant to work for other people and just open a business directly, Briana took the longer route. To gain more knowledge about the business, she applied to a spa and worked as a therapist for several months. But she realized that she kept trying to tell the boss how to do things better. Briana said, "Of course I was terribly annoying to her and she just always said to me, 'If you think you can do it better, you should do it yourself.' One day when I got fired, I thought to myself, 'I think I can do it better, so I will!'"

With zero capital to start with, she enlisted one of her former co-massage therapists as a business partner; something that she would strongly suggest against in the future. But at that time, she only had her focus on one thing: her own spa. Their initial fund of $50,000 was collected through the support of family and friends who saw her dedication to make her start-up business work. She wrote an extensive business plan with "really great projections and a lot of financial stability shown in it." Her business plan was her proof that she's in it to win it. She recalled how uncomfortable it was to request funding, as it is when asking money especially from family and friends, but her confidence that she would do everything to pay the money back, whether her idea worked or not, kept her afloat.

A 4,500-square-meter space fueled Briana's dream. But that space turned out to be too big for a spa that basically has a staff of two, herself and her business partner, as they didn't have enough money to hire more people, nor improve the facility. They were the massage therapists, receptionists, clean-up girls, and more. But they kept going. Nothing can put out a girl's raging fire of passion.

A year and a half into the business, Briana bought her business partner's shares. She views business partnership as getting "married" to that person, and if you don't share the same principles and dreams for the business, then the relationship is bound to fail. She wanted to take the spa to a higher level—marketing, expansion, and so on—while her business partner was just contented with a low-key existence. So when she had the chance to go solo and buy her partner's shares, she didn't hesitate to do it.

Running the spa business on her own allowed her to expand her horizons more. She applied for another loan to furnish more massage rooms, install showers and saunas, and hire more people. Her spa's growth didn't come at an easy cost, especially when it came to managing people. She was 22, and while the first few years of the business taught her a lot, she still had a lot to learn when it came to handling people. It is actually quite a feat for someone her age to run a business, plus be the boss of a staff no less than 10.

First, she had to do away with hiring people who only seemed "cool" but do not perform really well. As she was relatively young, she ended up getting people older than her and she felt as if she had to cater to them because of the age gap. She figured that as the boss, she should be more in control, without making her staff feel inferior. Problems cropped up every now and then, but her growing experience in management allowed her to take care of every situation well. She listened to her employees, and asked them for what they thought could be the best solution to a particular issue so she could gain their input. She realized that giving them ownership brings out their best, without you, the boss, compromising your leadership and control.

A few years after her first spa venture, an opportunity came again in the form of a spa space in the airport. While she clearly didn't ask for it, it was a chance she wouldn't easily let go as she finally had a wealth of knowledge under her belt. The space was smaller than her first branch but it didn't mean that Briana spent less time planning everything out. She poured all her energy into the new territory. Having the funds to furnish and improve the facilities and get the right people truly helped in establishing it. It was easier the second time around.

It was just two years earlier when an untimely injury opened up another business break for Briana. She was doing some massage sessions at a golf event, which she rarely does since she has tons of stuff on her hands, when a massage chair fell on her feet and badly hurt her ankle. Indeed, fate will pave the way when it has something great in store for you. In Briana's case, though, it was just a bit more painful. Her ankle swelled and hurt a lot and people had to carry her home. Good thing her husband, an acupuncturist and herbalist, knew of a concoction to alleviate her huge, painful, swelling ankle. A few hours after he applied it on her bad foot, the swelling was miraculously gone. Then the next day, it was as if nothing happened!

This sent the entrepreneur in Briana's brain—and her husband's—whirring again. With her husband's skill and support, she decided to venture into creating a pain patch to help others who feel various kinds of body pain. Briana always has it in her to reach out and help make people's lives easier and more convenient. In her business's case, more relaxed and less painful. When she and her husband were finally sure that they wanted the pain patch business to take off, they searched for a manufacturer who could make these patches, as it's more convenient that way. They found one in Taiwan and proceeded to seek the Food and Drug Authority's (FDA) approval.

As all plans go, they went through several obstacles first. They ran into an FDA shipping-related problem when the patches were sent to the United States. It took them six months to figure and work something out, which included countless e-mails and communication with the FDA officials. All these months of waiting never took their hope that things would eventually go through.

Marketing their pain relief patches was the next hurdle to surpass. If starting a business isn't hard enough, getting your product out there for the consumers is a more challenging task. Briana and her husband found themselves calling buyers and checking out every venue where they could market their innovative pain patch. They knew that the best way to do it was through Whole Foods, but people weren't eager to take them in. Finally, her husband, who was on a trip to Boston, gathered his guts and walked into a Whole Foods office, where he found a willing buyer to support them.

To future entrepreneurs, or basically to everyone who has this teeny-weeny spark of an idea going on in their heads, Briana advises to always plan ahead. She plans her next year at the start of the current year, no matter how advance-thinking that sounds. She says to list:

> 10 things that you really want in the next year and then actually put them on your calendar. Don't get sidetracked by other little things that might come up because it's really easy to have shiny object syndrome when you're an entrepreneur. If you already have a plan, you'll see whether that fits or not rather than just kind of being swayed by everyone else and other little things. You will get your bigger things accomplished and some of the smaller things really don't pay off anyway so it makes way more sense to just make sure that you are focusing on the things that are important and do that by putting them in your calendar.

Kane Minkus

Before: Homeless
Business: Jeff and Kane: Industry Rockstars

> I just remember thinking that this can't go on, and I don't know what the heck I am going to do, but something has got to change.
>
> —KANE MINKUS

Kane was a talented musician as a teenager. But at around 22 years old, he hit a turning point. "I was completely homeless and broke, $40,000 in debt, actually sleeping on a friend's couch wondering what the heck I was going to do with the rest of my life. I wondered why I was so broke when I had worked so hard throughout my teenage years as a musician and loved music and was supertalented. But I was totally, *totally* broke and didn't see any future, and I just didn't understand how to make money."

He might have kept going on that path, but he didn't. Instead he found a mentor. In fact, he met an amazing executive leadership coach by chance. He was one of the top coaches in Silicon Valley.

Kane didn't have any money to pay him, but the coach knew he was homeless and extremely passionate. "I met my coach at a Landmark event where he stood up and said, 'I just sold my media company in Los Angeles. I just moved back to San Francisco to executive coach with my parents,' and I said, 'Wow, perfect. I'm going to go talk to this guy.'

"So I went over, and I was real excited. I had just moved to LA. I had been living in Nashville and New York producing records. I said, 'I just started a music company. I have no idea how to run a company, but I really want this to be a success, because I have to prove my father wrong. There is money in music.'

"This guy was actually a musician as well. I think just out of the goodness of his heart and I always have to love him for that, he just said, 'Look, let me come down to your office and see what you're doing and what's going on.' I said, 'Cool, my office is my bedroom.' Within three years we created a company that became top five in the world in media."

The funny thing is, working with the coach wasn't like Kane had thought. His coach didn't just talk about how to market or sell. "He was directing my attention toward relationships and leadership skills and strategic skills. It was about a real deep connection, a heart connection to the people we were doing business with, to finding customers that we want to work with, to addressing our message as a company. I trusted that even though we were talking about squishy stuff that he had the credibility to have my ears to say maybe there is something else other than all the hard business stuff."

Kane went on to create many more companies, five of which are multimillion-dollar businesses. He said the skills and mind-set he gained is learnable and repeatable. He has worked with amazing business owners and even very popular celebrities. He said, "We've trained some major celebrities that everybody would know by name who have had massive exposure. They come to us because they are either broke or frustrated, thinking they should be making millions more with my exposure.

"Some are all over movies, and they're like but I'm not making any money. Or maybe they're making money, but they realize they should be making 10 times as much money for the amount of exposure they have. Exposure is very important once you have the products, once you're packaged up, once you're clear. Before then, it's totally useless. It's not going to get you anywhere. It's just going to get you exposure. It's selling products and services that actually make you money."

Kane has been able to teach many others the secrets to his success, but he doesn't seem like a "guru." He seems like a normal guy, doing what he loves.

Lewis Howes

Before: Professional Arena Football player
Business: Serial Entrepreneur and Author

> I had to find someone who could teach me this fast so I could make money. It was like a survival mode. "I need to get off my sister's couch. Can you show me how to do this so I could make money?"
>
> —Lewis Howes

Lewis was an athlete. He had worked his entire life to be a success in football. He started to play professionally in the Arena Football League, but one day his path hit a wall—literally. He injured his wrist by diving into a wall. He thought he could keep playing, but by the end of the season it was obvious that he could no longer play the game. He had worked toward that goal his whole life, and it was shattered. That type of event changes your life. He had to figure out what skills he had besides football, and he had to find a job because he had no money.

He said, "I had to have surgery on my wrist, and for six months I was in a full arm cast. I didn't have any savings; I didn't have a backup plan. I didn't get my college degree yet. And this was around 2008 when the economy was pretty bad, and people were just losing their jobs left and right. So who was going to hire a college dropout who had no internship experience and no degree during one of the worst economic downturns? I couldn't even do manual labor because I only had one good arm."

He ended up living on his sister's couch. He was eating macaroni and cheese. He admits he was getting depressed. But one day he had an epiphany. He wasn't going to let himself be depressed anymore. He became a student of business, and he used what he knew from sports about performance and discipline and incorporated those attributes into his business. He didn't have any money to start, so he had to start his business with a lot of hard work. He had gained many skills using LinkedIn when he had been looking for a job. He used those skills to start his business of teaching others how to use LinkedIn's resources and how to network. He also started to reach out to successful people to see what they were doing and what worked for them.

"I realized that there were some very interesting people on LinkedIn that I could connect with just to learn how they got to where they are in their career, or how they grew their business, or how they made millions. So I just started reaching out to people one by one asking them if I could ask them questions, if I could interview them, or meet them in person for breakfast, and just ask them how they got to where they are. I learned some very interesting things by interviewing these people or just meeting them in person."

Lewis had the desire to succeed and remove himself from the situation he was in. He was willing to do whatever it took. He would spend eight or more hours a day connecting with people and hustling to start to grow his business. Lewis wasn't an overnight success. But he was eventually able to get his own place, and his desire to succeed more was still there. So he continued to make progress. He said, "From May 2008 to May 2009, the only way I was really making any money was hosting these LinkedIn or sports-networking events. I would get around 300 to 500 people to show up in person to live three- to four-hour mixer networking events in different cities at a bar or a restaurant. We'd open up the space; people would just network and share business cards.

"I was originally doing them for free to see if I could get anyone to show up, because I had never done anything like it before. Then

I said, okay, why not charge $5 and see if people would still come. They still did. I charged $10, then $20, and they still came. Actually more people came and drove out the bottom feeders who didn't want to pay anything. So I was getting quality people when I started charging more.

"Then I wondered if I could get people to pay a sponsorship and sell a table. So I started selling tables for $250, and they would sell out. *Then,* because there were about 500 people at these events, and the venues were making a lot of money off all the alcohol and food sales, I wondered if I could ask them if I could get a percentage from that. So I was getting up to fifteen percent food and bar sales.

"I came out with my book in March 2009 about LinkedIn, and I was hosting these LinkedIn events. So I just had my own table and I was selling about a hundred copies of my book at each event. I was getting them for $2.50 and I was selling them for $10. So I was making all this good cash, but I was lugging around these boxes of books everywhere.

"It was good money, but it was a lot of work for me. I was starting to get burnt out. I had done 20 of these in a year, and I was like, man this is a lot of work for three or four grand cash. For me, I felt like I was making money finally, but it was still not where I wanted to be. It wasn't until I did my first webinar in May 2009 where I made $6,300 in one hour—and I had no clue what I was doing and I basically messed up the entire webinar—that I was in shock that I made that much money. At the time, I thought I was rich. I was like, I am going to retire. I'm freaking rich. I can do whatever I want now."

In four years, Lewis went from being on his sister's couch to running a million-dollar online business. Now he travels the world on his own schedule, works with his friends, and speaks at conferences, all while running his seven-figure business (and salsa dancing every chance he gets!).

Marissa Levin

Before: Trainer in the telecommunications industry
Business: Information Experts

Staying true to your core and what you believe in and what you believe your mission is what has been the secret to my success.
—MARISSA LEVIN

Marissa didn't expect to become an entrepreneur. In fact, she had a degree in English with a concentration in Shakespeare. She started working as a trainer in the telecommunications industry. She said, "After I put myself through a master's degree program in about 18 months, and I went in to really quantify my work to the owner of the company, he told me that I would never be worth more than $34,000 while I was working there. So he basically capped my worth at $34,000. It was just kind of a light bulb went off.

"It was at that time that I just decided that I was making him a lot of money. He was double-billing me and double-booking me on different projects, and I was bringing in clients. I was putting out great content, and I had a lot of value in the market, and I just decided that I could do this myself. That is really what gave me the motivation and proved to be the catalyst for me to start my own firm, Information Experts.

"When I did it, I really didn't know everything that I was biting off—I didn't know I was biting off more than I could chew. I knew I didn't want to work for a company that had the value system that my previous company had. I knew that I was worth a lot more. I had an idea of what I wanted my life to look like, and I just didn't see it happening where I was working.

"So it wasn't that I started a business with a grand vision of what I wanted; I was starting from a place of knowing more of what I didn't want and what wasn't working for me. I just felt that the only way that I could really create the future and the life that I wanted was to take ownership of it.

"That's basically how I started. My first contract was actually $35,000 in three months, so I made a $1,000 more in three months than I had been making in a year. After that first contract, things just started to roll, and I never looked back."

It took Marissa a while to grow into the amazing businesswoman she is today. She worked as the sole employee in her business for the first year, both selling and delivering her services. After her first year she realized that she couldn't do it all alone. She was wearing too many hats, and there weren't enough hours in the day for the amount of work she had. She progressed each and every year, all the time learning more about her business and herself, building an enterprise from that first $35,000 contract to projecting revenues of $15 million this year. It sounds like an amazing success story, but she's had issues along the way, too.

"One of the things that I tell people is that I have had to sacrifice the growth of my company for the development of my children—and that's okay. I would make those choices again in a heartbeat. You have to just really be gentle and kind with yourself and do all that you can do and not compare yourself to others and not get frustrated if things aren't moving as fast as you want them to move with the business, but just to trust the process and continue to try and enjoy the journey and stay focused on why you're doing what you're doing."

She still has issues to this day on that front, just like every other working mother. She needs to remind herself that her children are more important than the growth of her company. "I just reached out to a friend earlier in the week completely panicked that things weren't moving fast enough and that I'm pulled in a million directions, because I'm trying to get one of my kids through a transition to middle school, one ready for middle school, and one getting ready for high school. I get frustrated that I can't be here and I can't be there. My friend said to me, 'If things get delayed a year, you're still going to be okay. Your kids need your focus.'"

Ryan Eldridge

Before: Owned marketing company
Business: Nerds on Call

We quickly hired as many people as we could, and over the course of three to four months, we blew through our initial investment of $60,000. We blew through that just setting up the office and hiring staff. And from those three months on, we've been profitable ever since.

—RYAN ELDRIDGE

Ryan didn't initially set out to start a highly successful computer repair company. It hadn't even crossed his mind. He ran a website as well as his own marketing company and did well for himself in 2003. Things changed when he made the move to Northern California and the demand for his services decreased drastically. It wasn't until his mother-in-law got a virus on her computer that Nerds on Call was envisioned. "I went over and removed the virus, and she said to me, 'This is so great, shouldn't there be someone out there to come to your house to fix this stuff for technogoofs like me? Kind of like a plumber for your computer.' And I said that's a pretty great idea."

Ryan and his wife decided to place an ad in the local Redding, California newspaper simply stating that they were self-proclaimed nerds who were willing to travel and fix computers. They put Ryan's wife's cell phone number in the ad not expecting to get a huge response. They were sorely mistaken. "That ad came out on a Thursday, and by Friday we were booked for three solid weeks from 7 in the morning to 10 at night. Her first cell-phone bill was over three grand, simply because people kept calling."

Business began to grow with each passing day and Ryan realized that he couldn't carry the workload on his own. In the first three months, he hired additional staff to make house visits and fix computers and within a year, they had opened up a second location in Chico, California.

That's when the business took off. "After we broke through that wall or that ceiling, so to speak with the second location, we quickly opened up multiple locations. We opened our Sacramento office, just three months after the Chico office, and then we opened our Yuba City store. By 2007, we opened four stores in a row."

In 2007, although still profitable, Nerds on Call began to slow down and marketing prices started to rise. What was costing them $187.50 in marketing to acquire new business was only giving them a payout of $161.90 per new client. After crunching the numbers and realizing that they were losing money on new customers, along with new competition arising, Ryan posed the idea of changing the philosophy of his company. Instead of focusing on marketing to gain new customers, he decided to increase training of his staff and give unparalleled great customer service to ensure customer loyalty.

Before, the Nerds would only go if the computer had a tech issue. That all changed and they decided to adopt the philosophy of no job being too small and making sure the customer had the best experience possible. Even if someone's printer ran out of ink days later and they got a call, they wouldn't say no. No job was too small. "We said 'What's the big deal? Fix their printer.'" If they need ink, let's just go buy some ink, and put it in there and make them happy. And stop worrying about it being our fault, or them thinking we're doing bad things. I said if we walk away and say no to customers, they're always going to think badly."

Although some were apprehensive and feared they would be taken advantage of, they decided to test the waters and give people the great customer service. "We came up with this great idea of never say no to a customer. You have to have permission from a manager to say no to a customer. And, once we stated that policy, Wow! We went nuts! That's when we opened up the rest of our stores!"

Along with great customer service, the Nerds on Call website was designed for people to have an enjoyable experience if they need to have their computer fixed. It's filled with cartoon-like animated characters and is designed to make their customers feel more comfortable. It's all about the experience for the customer and making them feel okay that they don't have all of the answers. "There's only a few buttons to press, there's not a lot of stuff to get lost. It's very simple, very easy going. The cartoons are very cute, and funny and very nerd-esque. And we make it look like a comic book, and the idea was that we wanted to be very approachable."

In an ever-evolving world of computers, Ryan and his fellow Nerds have also changed with the times and are now working on a monthly service that can provide assistance to anyone around the nation. For a monthly fee, people will be able to subscribe and learn how to troubleshoot programs they use each and every day like Excel and Photoshop.

Ryan knows that without listening to his wife's suggestions, making lists to know where his money was going and a little bit of luck, Nerds on Call may never have flourished like it has. In the fast-paced world of computers and on-call tech support, Nerds on Call is still a highly successful service and doesn't look to be slowing down anytime soon.

Sue Ismiel

Before: Medical records keeper and mom of three
Business: Nad's Hair Removal

People had high expectations of me, and I had high expectations of myself. I always wanted to become someone and achieve something worthwhile, and I think that's helped me on this journey.

—Sue Ismiel

Sue was born in Syria and lived there with her family until she was 15 years old. Her father wanted a better life for their family, and so they decided to immigrate to Australia. Sue was the oldest and she was really excited. But there was a defining moment in her life that changed all of that excitement. "I encountered the most significant moment of my life on the third day of my arrival to this country. I was assaulted and bashed up on a school bus by a group of girls because I could not speak English.

"Every time I reflect on that moment, I almost see myself flat on my face embarrassed and humiliated. But you know, looking back at that defining moment in my life, I have nothing but gratitude for it, because I knew that there were only two options for me. I either had to learn the language and connect and become part of this new world that I'm in, or I could shrivel, wither, and die. I obviously didn't want to do that, so I had to do whatever necessary to become who I am today. It took me three months to learn the language, make friends, accept myself, and move forward in life."

That pivotal moment made Sue dive into learning the language, because nothing was more important. Her whole life depended on becoming a part of the Australian culture. She went on to live a typical life in Australia. She became a medical records keeper and had three daughters. Her middle daughter, Natalie, however, had inherited the worst part of her father—his very thick and dark hair. Even at only six years old, it became very apparent that the hair on Natalie's arms made her very embarrassed at school.

That didn't sit right with Sue. Knowing what it was like to feel alienated, she decided to do whatever it took to solve her daughter's problem. First she went through all of the normal products in the supermarket but was unhappy with all of them. So instead she decided to become, as she calls it, a mad scientist. She didn't have a scientific background nor any knowledge, so she worked on a concoction for more than 12 months. She learned as much as she could about different formulas and old homeopathic remedies.

Many times she thought to herself, "My gosh, I must be crazy for doing this. What am I doing?" But the very next day she would be at it again, trying to figure out something that worked. It was like an obsession. At the end of those 12 months she had this weird, all-natural green goo—that worked!

She tried to sell her product to bigger companies like Revlon or Avon, but they weren't interested. Sue decided she was going to make her product a success, whether or not they were going to help. She started cooking the goo called "Nad's" on her stove. The problem was she had no selling experience in her life. (In fact, when her kids brought fund-raising stuff home to sell, she would just buy a bunch herself instead of trying to sell it.) To try and sell her first batch, she and her sister decided to go and set up a stall at the local market. They stood there for three frustrating hours. They had their Nad's units displayed. They had their pink tablecloths. They went there hoping that they would make a killing.

Not one person approached them. Then she had the thought that no one really knew what this was, because they hadn't asked. She decided that she needed to be more vocal and tell them. She started to interact with people passing by. Some people looked at her like she was crazy. But others actually came up to learn more.

Before she knew it, she was doing demonstrations and shaping eye brows in the middle of the market. Then she sold out in less than an hour. She said, "I had never seen so much cash in my life. It was the most exciting moment in my life. So I knew that this was a winner. I just could not wait to get back to that spot again."

After she launched Nad's, one day she was doing a product demonstration when she met someone unexpected. "I saw this face in the crowd that I recognized, and my jaw dropped. I just stopped and froze, and then I walked toward her and I asked her, 'Is your name Faye?' She replied, 'Yes.' She was the leader of the girls who assaulted me on the bus that day. I said, 'Did you go to Fairfield Girls' High School?' She said, 'Yes.' I said, 'Do you remember me?' She said, 'No.'

"I felt like revenge. But then you know what? At that point in time I reflected on that present moment, on what I had become, and on what I was surrounded with, and I actually thanked her and forgave her and moved forward. I put that part of my life behind me, and I always look at it in a very positive way."

Sue set up another demonstration and then another, and ended up upgrading to shopping centers. Finally she took a leap of faith and started to advertise on television. That was the turning point of her business. She started to grow and grow. "I'll never forget the day that I picked up the phone and I called my dad and I said, 'Look, your efforts as a lab rat haven't been wasted, Dad. I'm on my way to becoming a millionaire.'

"My dad's response was, 'Ah, well, I'd love to live to see that day.' I can tell you that my dad is alive and proud." Nad's is a multimillion-dollar business, and Sue is now able to spend time doing what she loves. She is a huge giver and loves to spend time with her daughters helping others in need.

What You Can Do Now to Start Your Millionaire Journey

So here we are. You've made it to the last chapter of this book. We have covered a substantial amount of topics. You have heard not only my story, but the stories of millionaires who started with nothing more than an idea and slowly climbed their way up to the top. Sure, it took some of them a little while to obtain their goals, but this book is called *The Eventual Millionaire* and not *The Overnight Millionaire.* You're probably wondering, "What can I *do* now," and that's a great question. If you tried to do everything that was discussed in this book all at once, you'd probably burn yourself out within a matter of weeks.

I ask the same question at the end of every single interview I conduct: "What is *one* action readers can take this week to move them forward towards their goal of a million?" Following are the top 10 answers to the question.

Figure Out How to *Save* Money

> Figure out how you can save money. It's one thing to make money but you really start to amass wealth when you start to save and you see where you can save things.
>
> —DAN NAINAN

First thing is first. You need to figure out how to save money. We live in a world that is fueled by spending money and having the newest toys. If you have debt, you must pay it off before you can really start saving toward your goal. I started with $70,000 of debt and was able to pay it off. We made some major lifestyle changes and learned that even though we weren't living the high life, we were able to change our spending habits. It may seem difficult at first to put money away, but nearly everyone has areas in their life that they can change in order to live a less expensive life. Be sure that when you do make needed purchases, you make the most financially responsible choices.

Start Working with the Money You Have *Now*

To start a successful business and keep it running, you need to have a firm grasp on your finances and where your money is going. If you're in debt, do everything you can do to get out of it. Although it may seem like you do not have the funds necessary to start your business, with a little bit of maneuvering and budgeting, you should be able to find more funds you can use toward your goal. Maybe you don't need cable television. You could scale back on your data plan on your cell phone. Write down all of your expenses and see where you can cut back.

Remember the four debt-free rules. Rule #1: Be honest with yourself when it comes to finances. Rule #2: Be value-conscious with your money. Rule #3: Numbers in your head do not count. You must write them down in order to have a firm grasp on your finances. Rule #4: Control your money. Cut your expenses, sell unwanted items, do whatever it takes to make sure your finances are in complete control.

Action Item

Download the Eventual Millionaire Starter Kit at http://TheEventualMillionaire.com and fill out the worksheets to get in control of your money.

Find a Problem to Solve

Go and solve a problem. At the end of the day, it's hard to say I want to make a million bucks. It's easy to say I am going to create a business that's going to solve a real pain point. Try working on solving it and getting customers that are willing to pay for it. That's how you'll make your million dollars. You're not going to make a million dollars saying, "I want to make a million dollars. What do I need to make a million?" That's hard.

It's much easier to find a problem, solve it and the money will come if you are actually solving a real problem that people are willing to pay for.

—NEIL PATEL

Businesses are most generally started due to an issue that consumers have. Consumers have a dilemma and businesses fix that dilemma. Generally speaking, most businesses deal with products or a provided service (many times both) consumers need, or at least think they need. Find a problem that needs solving and build your business plan around the solution.

Before starting a business, there are some key steps you need to take to determine what business plan is actually worth your time and effort. By now, I hope you have realized the importance of carrying around a journal. Record all of your business ideas/evaluations in a journal. Create a list of at least 10 business ideas to start off. Go through and eliminate the business ideas that do not fit with your lifestyle or ability to fund the start-up costs. You may think that what you have is a great business idea, but if that idea does not fit with your life or you don't think you'll ever have the funds to get the business started, it's probably not the best idea to pursue right off. After you have determined which three business ideas fit your lifestyle and price range, create a SWOT analysis for the business ideas you have. Remember, SWOT stands for:

- Strengths: Characteristics of the business that give it an advantage over others.
- Weaknesses: Characteristics that place the business at a disadvantage relative to others.
- Opportunities: External chances to improve performance in the environment.
- Threats: External elements in the environment that could cause trouble for the business.

Action Item

Go buy a journal today or use an app like Evernote to keep track of your ideas. Write down at least 10 ideas today!

Differentiate Yourself from Your Competition

> Evaluate where your value is. Really sit down and break down your idea. Is there anything in there that beats the competition? If there is, can you get in front of the customer base that you need to? If you can, those are really the two things to figure out and if not, start over with a new project.
>
> —BILLY MURPHY

Your idea for a business may not be completely original, but the way you tackle the solution can be original. Differentiate yourself from your competition and explain why you have more to offer than everyone else. Think about being hungry in a busy city and coming across a group of food trucks. Each food truck offers different choices. Businesswise, they are all similar. They all offer food and drink, but they are all unique and offer different options that will ultimately solve your problem, an empty stomach. The same goes for differentiating yourself from your competition. You need to be able to prove to the general public that your products and/or services are better than your competition.

Once this is done, delve into the competition that exists so you can see a clear picture of what you are up against. Find out what they do in order to see what is unique about yourself. In fact, you may want to even contact the business and do research. Pretend you are a prospective customer and see how they cater to your needs. Use that information to create your business strategy.

Action Item

Identify your customer. You can't offer your product if you don't know who is your target audience. Find at least 5 to 10 of them, set up meetings with them, and get their honest feedback (and see if they can become customers now!).

Create a Mastermind Group

> You need a powerhouse team, because you are going to run up against not knowing what to do. And if you don't have the right mentors, right coach, right consultants, right design team, the right people helping you get there, understanding what your

goal is, and by the way, they should all be more successful than you are, if you don't have that, forget it. I really mean that. I mean, forget it. I've made this mistake so many times, and when I have powerful people around me, I get there a lot faster.

—AMY APPLEBAUM

Remember, a mastermind group is about four to seven of your peers. These people are different from your mentors. These are people just like you, working on their business. They're sharing current resources, tactics, and things that work for them, plus they give you support. They are the people you meet with regularly on a weekly or biweekly basis. If you don't know of any mastermind groups you can join right off, create your own. Find potential members whether locally or online and invite them to be a part of your group. The group should be as useful, if not more, for them as it is for yourself.

Before starting a business, make sure you are equipped with a mastermind group. Millionaires have help and swear by using mastermind groups to help them achieve their goals. Follow in their footsteps and it will not only help you grow, but will help them as well.

Look for a mastermind group of individuals who have similar interests. If you cannot find one, or there are none that exist close by, create a list of 20 possible members for your own mastermind group. Refer to Chapter 5 for an example e-mail that you can send to your peers, or those in your extended network. Mastermind groups are typically anywhere from four to seven people in size so don't expect all 20 to accept your request to join. Once you have established your mastermind group, make sure you set up a time to meet regularly. Most mastermind groups meet on a weekly basis and all of them have a specific agenda that they follow. Remember to plan out each meeting to ensure that the group stays on topic and is the most productive that it can be.

Action Item

Start asking friends and other business owners if they would be interested in a mastermind group with you. Reach out to people who are better than you in business. Ask them if they would be interested if you put a mastermind group together with other amazing business owners.

Find a Mentor

> If you can find someone that is willing to be your mentor, do whatever you can to impress their socks off so that they keep kicking your butt because then you're going to grow. You're going to keep progressing and you're going to get where you want to go. So before you even do that, you need to find out where it is that you want to go. Sit down, unless you can find someone that is going to do that for you, but you find a mentor that's going to guide you through the process of working out your plans.
>
> —Cindy Battye

Your mentor is a trusted adviser or guide. A mentor is not someone you need to meet with on a weekly basis, but it should be someone who you are able to talk to whenever needed. Remember, these are people who help push you out of your comfort zone, help with business strategies, and raise your confidence in your product and yourself. These are people who have qualities that you lack, and ones you want to improve upon.

Action Item

Create a list of 10 possible mentors. Look for those who know more than you do in your field of business, or in something that you are interested in learning more about. Find their e-mail addresses and e-mail them! You don't have to check in with them on a weekly basis, but the understanding is that these mentors are there for you when you have questions or need guidance. They have probably traveled the road that you are on and have insight into how to deal with the situation at hand.

Keep Learning

> One of my biggest fears in life is that I would wake up one morning and realize that I'm not learning anymore. I've stopped learning. I kind of subscribe to the fact that I'm always improving, I'm always learning more.
>
> —Adii Pienaar, Founder of WooThemes and PublicBeta

We live in an ever-changing world, and it's crucial to keep learning. Even if you are an expert in your field, there are plenty of opportunities to learn new aspects of business and how to best reach your target audience.

But not only that, growing personally will help you in your business. Learning how to work with your emotions, or your fitness and nutrition, or your relationships will help you be happier. (Which will transfer to your business—customers want to work with happy owners!)

Millionaires are constant learners, always seeking an improvement over what exists now, personally and professionally. The goal is to learn and then implement that learning as soon as possible.

Action Item

Choose one area of your life to learn more this week. It could be implementing something in your business, or it could be improving your health, or your spirituality. Pick one subject and dedicate this week to learning more about it, so at the end of the week, you know enough about a piece of it that you could teach someone else what you are learning about.

Focus!

> If you focus on making a million dollars, you might make a million dollars but I think you'll probably be less successful. Don't focus on the reward, focus on the goal.
>
> —GUY KAWASAKI

We live in a world with constant distractions. Set aside a time to work on your idea, turn off your phone, find a quiet place, shut the door, and focus on what you need to get accomplished.

Remember that one of your main goals with focusing is making sure you continuously move forward. Although you don't need to map out each step you are taking toward your goal, your **focus** must be on continuous forward motion. For all intensive purposes, you probably won't ever have every step lined up. The most important thing you can do in moving forward is making the best decision you can with the information you have. Make sure you pinpoint your focus. Using a flashlight to highlight slides on a projection screen does not work nearly as good as a laser pointer. Determining how much time you have and how many different things you can juggle while still being productive will help you focus. Are you focusing on too many things at once? Your business may have many aspects like sales, customer service, marketing, and accounting. If you spread yourself too thin, you will lose your focus and become less productive. Instead of multiple things, choose *one* thing from both your personal and business life that you can focus on.

Remember to be patient as you move forward. It may sound like the two are polar opposites, but they go hand in hand. Patience is powerful. We live in a now world where things need to be done quickly. We yearn for instant gratification and do not have time to wait. If you don't have patience while starting off your business, you are bound to set yourself up for failure. Think about the mind-set of an ultramarathon runner.

"Start slow and slow down." If you try to do everything right out of the gate and don't pace yourself, you will burn yourself out and your business will fall apart. Make sure you are patient and balance your daily commitments. If you have a family, chances are you will have to balance your time working on your business as well as spending time with your family. If you do not have balance, one of them will suffer. Use patience when making decisions. If you are faced with several choices and unsure of which road to take, remember to ask yourself, "Which one of these things would be better if I do it now, while I'm younger or while the opportunity is fresh?"

Action Item

Implement focus now: Grab your to-do list right now. Is there anything on that list that you can cross off right now? Look at each item and ask yourself these questions:

- Do you want to do it?
- Will this bring you closer to your goal or vision?

If not, cross it off! Then choose three of the top priorities that you can focus on getting done this week.

Create, Write, and Be Accountable to Your Goals

> Absolutely have clear goals. I talk to so many people who have fuzzy goals. If you want to have a better job, what are your action steps over the next 48 days? What are you going to do specifically? If you want to lose weight, what are you going to do? Deciding and doing are two different things. A lot of people set goals but they don't achieve them. The reward is not in setting goals, that's a starting point. The real reward is in achieving them. So have clear plans for how you are going to achieve your goals.
>
> —DAN MILLER

Create a goal and write it down. Set a timetable for that goal to be met. Realistically speaking, if you set too many goals at once, you'll undoubtedly end up disappointed or burned out in a very short amount of time. Although you may think that simply having goals will be enough, writing down the goals will help ensure that you stick to them. Put your goals in a place where you'll look at them often. Tell your mentors your goals. Do whatever it takes to make sure you stay accountable to the goals you set up for yourself.

Your success is a series of accomplished goals. Set your goals using the COVENANT framework.

- Commitment
- Organized
- Values/Vision
- Enlightened
- Noticeable
- Accountability
- Numerical
- Time

Create your action plan, plus download the worksheet to help you. Take your written goal and break it up into several microgoals. Set specific timelines for yourself. Determine how many clients you want to meet with each week. If you have a website, plan guest posts to help bring in traffic. Set up timelines, whether they are in 30-, 60-, or 90-day increments. The purpose of creating an action plan is not so you can predict every single step that you will take. It doesn't matter how much you plan, the unpredictable will happen. Create an action plan so you can look back at the short-term results so you can better plan for the future.

Action Item

Create your millionaire routine. Start thinking about what habits you could be doing every day. What habits will help you get closest to your goals? Set a reasonable amount of time to work on your business goals, read this book, and take action. Find out what habits you need to start in order to achieve your goal. Refer to page 201 and list what your millionaire routine will look like. Stick to that goal and remember, always strive for continuous forward motion.

It's All about Sales

At the end of the day, the math is simple. No sales equals no profits, which equals a failing business. While there are many aspects of a business plan, sales are primarily what will keep your business afloat. Without sales, you probably won't stay in business for very long unless you are plugging in your own money to keep the business running. You may need to put money into your business with initial start-up costs, but if you aren't generating sales, your business will more than likely fail.

Business Plans Are for Banks

Most of the millionaires who I have interviewed have either not had a business plan at all, or created one, but went with a nontraditional route. Although a 30-page business plan can be useful, it can also hinder you from actually pursuing your goal. If you haven't taken the time to write a full-blown business plan, that's okay. In fact, it's probably best that you haven't yet. Unless you have a business degree, or have done a fair amount of research, writing a 30-page plan will not be worth your time. Instead of attempting to write a traditional business plan, take these steps toward determining the different aspects of your business.

Brainstorm your reason *why*. Why is this product or service useful for the general public? What does it entail that other companies' don't? Then take your brainstorm ideas and write down the reasons it helps people.

Start to play with possible mission statements. Your mission statement will let potential clients know exactly what you stand for. Write down 5 to 10 and see which ones feel better. Ask your mentors and mastermind group what their opinion is and determine which one fits your business best.

Choose three key performance indicators. A key performance indicator is a number you can look at and determine whether your business is doing well. These numbers can include quantities like gross profit, net profit, number of new prospects, number of products sold, and several other determining factors. Using these indicators will allow you to see which areas are succeeding, and which ones need improvement. Set a specific time period and compare the actual numbers to your anticipated projections.

Create your sales and marketing launch strategy. Remember that while sales and marketing go hand in hand, they are very different. Create a sales pitch based on the information you have learned about your prospective customers. Get comfortable, ask questions, and find out what they need. Use the information you have collected to dollarize, and find a win-win situation. Use your resources and access to prospects (potential customers), network with others, utilize the skills you already have, and don't be afraid to ask for advice. Also, remember that selling a product online versus selling in person takes two different sales pitches. Learning how to pitch in person is a valuable skill and one that can be easily overlooked.

There is no such thing as a one-size-fits-all solution for marketing. Whether you realize it or not, consumers are being reached in a number of different ways both online and offline. Remember these four steps when determining a marketing strategy.
  Step #1. Look at competitors.
  Step #2. Look for current possible strategies that might work for your industry.
  Step #3. Choose the most likely options.
  Step #4. Choose a marketing testing strategy.

Action Item

Challenge yourself to sell something today. It doesn't have to take weeks. Even if you only have an idea, sell someone on your idea! Every business starts with the first sale. And every business grows with more and more sales. Step out of your comfort zone today and sell something.

Execute! Take Action! Just *Do* It!

Just take action. Go ahead and intellectualize it, strategize it but take an action. I'll add to that form a habit that if that habit is repeated will take you towards your goal. That's something I'm really getting more and more focused on in my coaching work is you take a goal and you break it down and you structure it to the base habits you need in order to achieve the goal so the goal becomes inevitable. Grab that habit and adopt one, just one habit.

—Todd Tresidder

The three things that you will probably run into before taking the plunge into your endeavor are struggles with fear, excuses, and confidence. Don't let these be a hindrance to your goals. Rather than being bogged down by the "What Ifs" of life and succumbing to your own fear and excuses, embrace them, harness them, and turn them into something that will create a positive outcome to your efforts.

Fear is a good thing. Fear allows us to understand where our comfort zone lies and when we need to overstep those boundaries. In business, fear takes many shapes and forms. It could be a fear of taking the first step toward a goal. It could be something simpler, like being an introvert and going to speak in front of a large audience about your product. Fear can be a motivator to protect you from making a bad business decision. Although it may seem like fear is negative, when used correctly, it can be a vital part of your steps toward reaching your goal. However, too much of a good thing can be a bad thing. Too much fear within a business can lead to failure. I have yet to meet a millionaire who is absolutely fearless. Fear of the unknown is in our human nature. Harnessing that fear and stepping beyond comfort zones is crucial for a successful business. A person with a fear of public speaking would find it easier to stand in front of people after doing it for six months straight. Fear can motivate us, or it can tear us down.

Excuses are often just a way for us to get out of something we don't feel comfortable doing. Excuses generally come hand in hand with fear, and can put a serious damper on reaching the goals we set for ourselves. The most common excuses related to business endeavors are: "I don't have any time!," "I don't have enough money!," and "I don't know how!" If you try and make an idea a reality but only use excuses of why you can't, you will never get your business off the ground and running. Aside from removing these excuses from your vocabulary all together, remember the three tools to get past your fear and stop the excuses.

Step #1: Recognize the fear.
Step #2: Harness the fear.
Step #3: Expand your comfort zone.

Remember, your comfort zone can grow. Just because you have a fear of something right now does not mean it will stay the same forever. Step out of your comfort zone and do it often. Your original fears will not be nearly as scary as they once were. Expanding your comfort zone will help you not only adapt to many situations you may come across in business, it will also help increase your confidence.

Confidence plays a key role in any successful business. The amount of confidence you have can and probably will determine the amount of success your business will have. You may not have a ton of confidence in yourself or your ability to start a successful business, and that's normal. Many millionaires had a lack of self-confidence when they first started. The key is the ability to change and become more confident. Becoming more confident takes practice, and as we know, practice makes perfect. You won't be an expert at pitching ideas to potential clients if you have never tried before. Practice pitching ideas and it will become more natural for you. The more you do something, the more confident you will become.

Remember that the opinion of others is important, but it should not wreck the confidence in yourself. After all, not everyone will necessarily agree with your idea, and they are entitled to their opinions. An opinion is a viewpoint that someone has that may not even be factual. Remember that when people give you advice. Be open to criticism, but do not let the naysayers get you down. This idea you have is yours and yours alone. Don't let the negative views of others destroy your confidence!

There's something you need to remember about business and life in general. No matter how much you plan, you will never be 100 percent ready to take on something new. Sure, you might be 90 percent ready, but there is still that 10 percent that is looming. At some point, you will have to take action and jump in with both feet. Sure, it's scary. It can also be the best thing you have ever done in your life. If you have taken the correct steps in preparing, *Do It!*

Action Item

Think of one area about which you are feeling fear. Implement one of the techniques mentioned in this book (Worst-Case Scenario, Just Jump, Set a Date, or Logically Counteract It) to get past it.

Closing Thoughts

Now you may be looking at this list of things and wondering how you are going to do everything at once. The short answer is, you don't. You aren't expected to do everything all at once. If you took on all 10 of these tasks in a matter of a few short days, you'd fail. Focus on the one or two actions that are most important to the success of your business.

You are reading this now, and will most likely put the book away once you finish these next few sentences. Did you get everything you needed before you leave? Go back through the action items in the book. If there is one thing that truly stands out for you as the next step, do it.

In closing, I'd like to leave you with the words of several people who have been through this process in the past and are now millionaires. At the conclusion of my interviews, I ask the same question to everyone.

What's one action that people can take this week to help move them forward to their goal of a million?

Here are some examples of the most common answers I received:

I guess it's really just to take a step. Actually put yourself out there. I mean another definition of entrepreneur is risk taker, in my opinion. You have got to take some risks. Take some calculated risks. Don't go crazy. Take some calculated risk. Put yourself out there and those that take risks are usually rewarded. That's the difference. If you've got an idea, you got a plan, tell somebody about it. If they're still telling you it's a great idea, keep moving it forward until you hit a roadblock or a hurdle. When you hit it, identify what it is, go back to those same people who got you to this roadblock, discuss it with them and see if they can help you solve to get around it. That's what I do. Keep moving forward, take chances, believe in yourself, trust your gut but be smart about it.

—BRENTON HAYDEN

I won't say be fearless because fear sometimes is just a motivator, but take that fear and put it aside and follow your dream anyway. You're not too old, you're not too young, you're not too shy or too poor or too anything. There are obstacles. We're always going to have obstacles but just put aside your fears and just go for it.

—ANITA CROOK

I'd have to say the belief in that it's possible. Never look back, keep moving forward and know that the person that made it before you, they put their pants on one leg at a time just like you. They're no better, no different than you. Many people have done it before you. Many people are going to do it after you. You can do it.

—KEVIN KAUFMAN

Because being an Eventual Millionaire is about the process more than the goal, make sure that you are taking the best next steps. And if you do that, and actually enjoy those next steps, and enjoy your family and life while you are doing the next best step, you have achieved success. You never know what that end goal will be like, but as long as you are doing what you feel is right, right now, and enjoy as much as you can, you have found it.

It's an amazing life. Have fun with yours.

Make sure to go to TheEventualMillionaire.com to get access to all of the Millionaire interviews or to sign up to receive an e-mail each week when a new millionaire interview comes out live.

Go to http://EventualMillionaire.com/StarterKit to download the starter kit and worksheets, and go to http://EventualMillionaire.com/BookBonus to get the extra bonuses!

Thank you, and keep moving forward!

About the Author

Jaime Tardy is a business coach and the owner of EventualMillionaire .com. Jaime has interviewed more than 100 successful millionaire entrepreneurs in a quest to find out how they did it. After leaving the corporate world and climbing out of more than $70,000 in debt, Jaime has come to realize that money doesn't matter much if you don't enjoy your work.

Jaime has been featured on CNN, MSN, and Yahoo! Finance.

She resides in the middle of nowhere in Maine, where she lives a blissful life with her two adorable kids, her contortionist, performance artist husband, and their absurdly happy dog, Sydney.

About the
Companion Website

To access the Eventual Millionaire Starter Kit and watch all of the interviews with millionaires, go to http://TheEventualMillionaire .com.

You will also find bonus gifts and material there. Enjoy!

Index